t
Prayer
of
Revenge

Doug Schmidt

NE✗GEN®

An imprint of Cook Commun
Colorado Springs,

NexGen is an imprint of
Cook Communications Ministries, Colorado Springs, Colorado 80918
Cook Communications, Paris, Ontario
Kingsway Communications, Eastbourne, England

THE PRAYER OF REVENGE
© 2003 by Doug Schmidt

First Printing, 2003
Printed in the United States of America

1 2 3 4 5 6 7 8 9 10 Printing/Year 07 06 05 04 03

Editor: Craig Bubeck, Senior Editor

Unless otherwise noted, Scripture quotations are taken from the *Holy Bible: New International Version®*. Copyright © 1973, 1978, 1984 by International Bible Society. Used by permission of Zondervan Publishing House. All rights reserved.

Library of Congress Cataloging-in-Publication Data

Schmidt, Doug.
  The prayer of revenge : forgiveness in the face of injustice / by Doug Schmidt.
     p. cm.
  ISBN 0-7814-3942-6 (pbk.)
  1. Revenge--Religious aspects--Christianity. 2.
Retribution--Religious aspects--Christianity. 3. Forgiveness--Religious
aspects--Christianity. 4. Prayer--Christianity. I. Title.
  BV4627.R4S35 2003
  234'.5--dc21
                                   2003000386

Dedication
To my wife, Linda

In Memory
To our son, Gregory

19th Century prayer offered after the death of a young son . . .

O God, to whom I am left to mourn his departure,
grant that I may not sorrow as one without hope
for my beloved who sleeps in you;
but, as always remembering his courage,
and the love that united us on earth,
I may begin again with new courage
to serve you more fervently
who are the only source of true love and true fortitude;
that when I have passed a few more days
in this valley of tears and this shadow of death,
supported by your rod and staff, I may see him face to face,
in those pastures and beside those waters of comfort
where I believe he already walks with you.
O Shepherd of the sheep,
have pity on this darkened soul of mine.

—Edward White Benson
written on the death of his son, Martin, in 1877

Endorsements

"There is no question in the Christian life more urgent to ask and more difficult to answer than this: 'How can we forgive our enemy and still uphold God's demands for justice?' Doug Schmidt gives us a biblical answer and does so superbly. His book is slim and his message is clear. An ideal combination."

Dr. Lewis Smedes,

author of the Christian classic, *Forgive and Forget*

"What do you do when you've been done wrong? Doug Schmidt helps you respond, not react out of your pain. Only the grace of forgiveness in the face of evil will set you free. Now, be set free."

Dr. Tim Clinton

President, American Association of Christian Counselors

"There is no issue that grabs my time more than forgiveness. Doug has hit on this great issue with a prophetic voice. If the leaders of the world would grasp what he's saying, we'd all live in a better place. If you want to forgive someone and you're having a hard time doing so, this book is for you."

Rich Hurst, Pastor of Adult Ministry at McLean Bible Church

Author of *Courage to Connect*

"What are we to do when someone shatters our lives and doesn't look back or even care? Doug Schmidt's book, *The Prayer of Revenge* wisely and clearly guides the reader through the flooding torrent of emotions and thoughts, as well as providing some specific action steps so that we are not overcome by evil, but learn to overcome evil with good."

Leslie Vernick

Director of Christ-Centered Counseling

Author of *How to Act Right When Your Spouse Acts Wrong*

"*The Prayer of Revenge* is an overwhelmingly honest depiction of how God views vengeance, justice, and forgiveness. I am amazed at the level of clarity with which Doug is able to intertwine biblical passages with every day experiences. It's my hope that the readers of this book will experience a catharsis as they begin to hear from the Lord about responding to injustice in their own lives."

Wanda G. Anderson

General Counsel, The Orchard Foundation

Member of The National Black Evangelical Association &

The New York Bar

"This astute book deals honestly and compassionately with the sense of unfairness, the passion for retribution, the struggle to forgive, and the flood of emotions that engulf and pull down even the most dedicated Christian who has suffered injustice. Interspersed with captivating stories, *The Prayer of Revenge* is a straightforward, biblically-solid, helpful discussion of a tough-to-handle topic."

Dr. Gary R. Collins, President of The Bridge Institute,

and author of *Christian Counseling: A Comprehensive Guide*

****

About the author . . .

Doug Schmidt is an editorial manager with Cook Communications and has been involved in Christian publishing for over 14 years. He has degrees in biblical studies and systematic theology from Wheaton College and Trinity Evangelical Divinity School. Doug was also a contributor to *The Quest Study Bible* — a best-selling resource that tackles some of the most difficult and provocative questions asked by contemporary readers of the Bible. For more information, visit www.dougschmidt.com

Disclaimer

Apart from the stories that are clearly identified as direct quotes, news events, or the author's personal experience, all of the anecdotes and illustrations in this book are fictional. Any resemblance to any person, living or dead, is purely coincidental. You will find several such stories in this book because sometimes biblical truths are better understood when they're seen in narrative form than when they're plainly stated.

The author holds to a Christian worldview that assumes an inspired and authoritative view of Scripture—namely, that all of the biblical writers were supernaturally-guided by the Spirit of God. Consequently, the message of the Bible, in its entirety, is consistent and free from logical contradiction. Because of this, we are better able to comprehend the difficult passages in Scripture by looking at similar, but easier-to-understand passages.

Many of the characters in the stories, anecdotes, illustrations, and even some of the biblical passages do not share this worldview. The author assumes that some of the readers of this book will not either— that is expected and welcome.

> *Read not to contradict . . .*
> *nor to believe and take for granted . . .*
> *but to weigh and consider.*
> —*Sir Francis Bacon*

As the title implies, this book focuses (in part) on the volatile topic of revenge. Keep in mind, however, that there is nothing in this book that would ever encourage the reader to do anything violent, immoral, vindictive, or illegal.

The supreme underlying message of this book is that every individual is responsible for his or her own thoughts, words, decisions, and actions . . . and that he or she will be judged accordingly—in this life and the next.

Acknowledgments

Since the principal response encouraged by this book is genuine acknowledgement, it's probably best that I admit my indebtedness here.

- To my family, for their sense of humor, support, and encouragement

- To my friends who offered candid and clarifying feedback during every stage of this project

- To my co-workers, who are the reason I love going to work every day

- To devoted men and women, those still living and those gathered to our ancestors, whose spiritual gifts continue to highlight and fill my spiritual gaps

- And finally to Him in whom we live and move and have our being . . . apart from whom, I could do nothing.

Bibliography

Allender, Dan, *Bold Love*. (Colorado Springs: NavPress, 1992).

Dumas, Alexandre, *The Count of Monte Cristo*. Translated with an Introduction and Notes by Robin Buss (Penguin Press 1996. Copyright in translation © Robin Buss 1996).

Grisham, John, *The Testament*. (New York: Doubleday, 1999).

Lewis, C. S., *God in the Dock*. © C. S. Lewis Pte. Ltd. 1970.

Lewis, C. S., *The Screwtape Letters*. © C. S. Lewis Pte. Ltd. 1942.

Lewis, C. S., *The Weight of Glory*. © C. S. Lewis Pte. Ltd. 1949.

Mundy, Linus, ed. *A Man's Guide To Prayer*. (New York: Crossroad Pub. Co., 1998).

Schmidt, Douglas C., "Demanding Justice, Finding Forgiveness" *Proclaim*. October 21, 2001.

Schmidt, Douglas C., "Do You Own or Rent Your Faith?" *Proclaim*. March 3, 2002.

Smedes, Lewis, *Forgive and Forget*. (San Francisco: Harper, 1984).

Van Loon, Preston, *A Cognitive Development Intervention for Clergy: Forgiveness Education*. (Ann Arbor: UMI, 1998).

Vincent, Richard, "The Imprecatory Psalms" © Richard J. Vincent, November 27, 1997.

Contents

Introduction

One of the deepest of all human emotions is the internal need for acknowledgment and vindication when a person has been unjustly harmed, injured, or wronged — and the offender feels no remorse whatsoever. In many of these cases, forgiveness seems impossible, if not wrong.

Let's begin with a story . . .

RON WRAPPED THE FIRST FISH with his recent exceptional-performance review, and filed both in the office cabinet drawer under "Career Development."

Earlier in the day, Ron's boss could hardly look him in the eye when he terminated Ron's position. "The CEO wants us to cut staff so the numbers will look better for the board meeting on Monday. Frankly, I think he's looking for a scapegoat—we both know what he's up to. But there's nothing I can do, so you need to be cleared out by 3:00. Security is now in your office taking your computer—hopefully you don't have anything too personal on it. I don't have a severance package for you because the Securities & Exchange Commission will think that the company is acknowledging some sort of liability. The SEC will probably contact you next week—no one's going to cover for you here, so you're better off just keeping your mouth shut. After the holiday, I'll see if Human Resources can help you with outplacement. But if The Big Guy decides to make you The Fall Guy, HR is not going to be much help. The whole thing just stinks."

Alone in his office for the last time, Ron wrapped the second fish in the CEO's "Vision for the Future" memo, and filed both under "Data for the Annual Report." For good measure, he put a pen with the company's logo in the fish's mouth.

"Yep, it's gonna stink alright," Ron chuckled nervously to himself as he wiped his eye with the back of his hand. After putting a picture of his kids in the last box, he slammed the fish-laden filing cabinet shut and locked it. Taking one last look at the place he'd invested the last 15 years of his life, he tossed the filing cabinet key behind his desk and went home.

Three months later, Ron could not believe the course of events that turned this situation around for him. But the emotional roller coaster he endured for those 90 days was something he would not wish upon his worst enemy—with the exception, perhaps, of his former CEO.

THIS IS A BOOK ABOUT RESPONDING TO EVIL—specifically, the type of evil that calls itself good. When confronted, the people who commit this type of evil are genuinely puzzled as to why you are upset. Imagine telling the soup kitchen worker that she's selfish for helping the homeless, or the neighbor that he's wrong for cutting an elderly couple's lawn. These generous people will probably look at you funny and wonder what you're talking about. You'll get a similar, yet twisted response from the drug dealer who insists he's just a businessman, or the wife beater who insists that "she had it comin'," or the cult leader who was "just making sure that nobody lost their salvation."

> Woe to those who call evil good
>
> —Isaiah 5:20

And because this type of evil views itself as justified, even noble, the people who embrace it tend to be unrepentant and remorseless. Like the helpful soup kitchen worker or the caring neighbor (who are actually doing good), the arrogant offenders see no reason to recant.

And then to our utter amazement, as we form a response to this type of evil, we think about crossing the line. We toy with the idea of abandoning the accountability and restraint of legitimate justice, and consider taking matters into our own hands. Gradually, we find ourselves calling this type of vengeful thinking justified and good — and suddenly we've become the thing that used to repulse us.

Many human emotions run very deep. Few feelings are so absorbing, however, as the internal need for acknowledgement and vindication when a person has been unjustly harmed, injured, or wronged . . . and the offender either gets away with it or gets off too easily — and feels no remorse whatsoever.

In most works of fiction there is no more popular source of conflict and need for resolution than a harmful injustice committed by a remorseless villain. And whether we encounter this tension in a book, a movie, or worst of all, in our own lives, we perceive that something is out of balance. It's as if our sense of emotional equilibrium has been thrown off-kilter. The pain of injustice we're seeing or experiencing makes us say, "This cannot be ignored, discounted, or excused away . . . the person who did this needs to be held accountable and face the appropriate consequences. This needs to be made right."

Many characters in the Bible, since they were human beings with deep feelings just like us, also struggled with this nagging sense of emotional disequilibrium when they experienced injustice. This is probably the most true of King David, whose explicit, and sometimes raw feelings are described quite passionately in many of the Psalms. Some of these passages are called the "imprecatory psalms" or David's "prayers of revenge." Surprisingly, over twenty-five percent of the psalms have some sort of appeal for justice and vindication in them.

> "It was fourteen years since Dantes' arrest. He was nineteen when he entered the Chateau d'If; he was thirty-three when he escaped. A sorrowful smile passed over his face; he asked himself what had become of Mercedes [Dantes' fiancé], who must believe him dead. Then his eyes lighted up with hatred as he thought of the three men who had caused him so long and wretched a captivity. He renewed against Danglars, Fernand, and Villefort the oath of implacable vengeance he had made in his dungeon. This oath was no longer an empty threat."
> —*The Count of Monte Cristo* by Alexandre Dumas

In these prayers, David does not hold back on how angry he feels or what he wants to see happen to those who provoked these feelings of rage. Since there's no recorded response from God to these prayers, Christians have been at a loss as to how to interpret, much less apply these Psalms. But we will see through God's response to similar prayers from other Old and New Testament saints that, under certain circumstances, God responds positively to these types of petitions and promises to act upon them.

So how do you know when it's appropriate to offer up a prayer asking for retribution? What's hazardous about offering such a prayer with a heart that's not ready? What can you expect to happen to you internally—emotionally and spiritually—after offering prayers such as these?

These are just some of the difficult questions that we'll address in the following pages. The essential key point to remember is this:

Your ability to forgive anyone, especially the unrepentant, is directly tied to your emotional confidence in God's willingness to accomplish justice on your behalf.

If you're reading this book because you're struggling with the ability to forgive someone, it's our hope that you will find that freeing capability in these pages—perhaps in a surprising place where you may have never looked.

1 Face-to-Face with the Eternally Remorseless

The "fool" that Solomon frequently describes in the Book of Proverbs represents the epitome of the remorseless offender. At best, fools angrily demand conformity to their agendas—at worst, they consume and destroy those who are slow or refuse to comply. While we must never label anyone as beyond redemption, some fools appear to be utterly incapable of accepting personal responsibility for their actions, and many will prove to be eternally resistant to change.

One summer I worked for a carpenter whose nickname for me was "Expendable." He'd say things like, "Hey, Expendable, clean up this mess so we can put the boards here." Surprisingly, as I worked with this man, I came to realize that this seasoned woodworker didn't have an ounce of mean-spiritedness in him. He laughed all the time, and I really enjoyed working with him.

But he kept calling me "Expendable," at least once or twice a week.

One day at lunch, when I was picking some sawdust out of my baloney sandwich, I asked him why he gave me such an endearing nickname. In the past, he had had to supervise several "kids" my age who had acted like they were doing him a favor by working for him. So, he just got into the habit of calling all of them "Expendable"—just to remind them how easily they could be replaced.

After that conversation, the diminutive tag disappeared, and he turned out to be one of my first mentors and a great friend.

In contrast, sometimes certain people come into our lives who never take responsibility for their insensitivity, much less stop what they're doing. In their minds, everybody's expendable. Some of them seem to delight in making others feel uncomfortable and have absolutely no interest in generating good will. When we become entangled with these people, either through work, school, or even in our families, life can become disturbingly unpredictable.

I've heard that it's common for the wives of alcoholics to keep attending the funeral of their husbands, in their minds at least, over and over again. To them, this final ceremony represents the long-awaited welcome end to years of abuse, emotional chaos, empty promises, and financial uncertainty. In these fantasies, the cause of death is usually liquor-related—either alcohol poisoning, cirrhosis of the liver, or a car accident where no one else is injured. They keep repeating this mental exercise because it has a calming effect on them—they can finally picture themselves in a stress-free environment, able to start life all over again.

We cannot assume that Nabal (in 1 Samuel 25) was an alcoholic just because his life ends shortly after a drunken stupor. But, from what we can tell from the story of his near-fatal encounter with David, he represented the worst that irresponsible and abusive personalities can bring to a marriage.

> *Now Samuel died, and all Israel assembled and mourned for him; and they buried him at his home in Ramah.*
>
> *Then David moved down into the Desert of Maon. A certain man in Maon, who had property there at Carmel, was very wealthy. He had a thousand goats and three thousand sheep, which he was shearing in Carmel. His name was Nabal and his wife's name was Abigail. She was an intelligent and beautiful woman, but her husband, a Calebite, was surly and mean in his dealings.*
>
> *—1 Samuel 25:1-3*

David had been on the lam for months—living in the wilderness, hiding in caves, and just barely escaping death by the hand of Saul (Israel's first king). Saul had long lost his sense of dependence on God, and his obsession with self-preservation was pushing him to the brink of insanity. Apparently, Saul's insecurity about David began when the people of Israel began attributing greater military victories to the former shepherd than to the king (1 Sam. 18:8). The prophet Samuel had given up on Saul, so there was no word from the Lord to comfort the increasingly paranoid ruler. The only thing that seemed to bring Saul any peace was David's harp playing—and, even then, the king's poorly-thrown spear had eliminated this only remaining source of consolation.

Now Samuel was dead, so the only person who would vouch for David was gone—the only one with any divine authority, that is. David had accumulated several loyal followers during this time as a fugitive, but most of them were considered outlaws too. After just barely escaping from Saul a second time, David was a man on the edge. This was the context when David and his men heard about Nabal's servants in the fields.

> *While David was in the desert, he heard that Nabal was shearing sheep. So he sent ten young men and said to them, "Go up to Nabal at Carmel and greet him in my name. Say to him: 'Long life to you! Good health to you and your household! And good health to all that is yours!*
>
> *" 'Now I hear that it is sheep-shearing time. When your shepherds were with us, we did not mistreat them, and the whole time they were at Carmel nothing of theirs was missing. Ask your own servants and they will tell you. Therefore be favorable toward my young men, since we come at a festive time. Please give your servants and your son David whatever you can find for them.'"*
>
> *When David's men arrived, they gave Nabal this message in David's name. Then they waited.*
> *—1 Samuel 25:4-9*

Now the sight of ten sinewy warriors coming over the hill must have been quite frightening for Nabal's shepherds. It was common in those days for groups of marauders to come sweeping down on unarmed field hands and simply take whatever they wanted. Sometimes they humiliated, tortured, or even killed these servants to let the owner know that their death squad was out there, and there was a price to be paid if the owner wanted his employees and livestock to be left alone. For this reason, shepherds feared gangs like these more than a starving pack of wolves.

David probably anticipated their uneasiness, so he told these ten representatives to greet the shepherds in David's name. One of the biggest reasons Saul was trying to hunt David down was because all of Israel knew that David was going to be the next king. So, these shepherds likely would have known who David was, and they would be set at ease by the impending authority behind the message that these ten men brought.

David's message could have easily been one of intimidation—*give us what we want, or we'll take more than you'd ever willingly give us.* Instead, David begins to show his leadership wisdom, and paints a picture where Nabal can *voluntarily* help David out, without appearing to be unduly pressured. David's message to Nabal, via the shepherds, was one of peace and a reasonable request for supplies.

Nabal's servants were not harassed or bothered by David's men, when they could have easily been mistreated. There is even a hint here that David's group was providing a degree of protection for Nabal's servants so that they would not be hassled by other less-than-gracious groups. David was so sure of the good behavior of his men (a reflection of their growing loyalty to him), that he called upon Nabal's servants to vouch for him and his cohorts.

After the message had been delivered, David's men held their ground and waited for the reply. There was no reason for David to expect that he would be denied.

It's common for good-natured people to be naïve about evil, especially for those who have never really encountered it. And even when they do come face-to-face with it, many think, "Certainly no one could be this cold and uncaring."

Some of them misunderstand what it means to "turn the other cheek," and so, these warm-hearted people continue to make themselves vulnerable to these remorseless types of people, only to get slapped—repeatedly. They just keep absorbing and absorbing, thinking that reciprocation is just around the corner. Some say to themselves, "If I can only find out what he really wants and make him happy, everything will be fine." But these attempts are never quite good enough, and the "give and take" of a normal, happy relationship never happens. Everyone, however, has a saturation point where nothing more can be absorbed. David doesn't know it yet, but he's about to reach that limit.

> *Nabal answered David's servants, "Who is this David? Who is this son of Jesse? Many servants are breaking away from their masters these days. Why should I take my bread and water, and the meat I have slaughtered for my shearers, and give it to men coming from who knows where?"*
>
> *David's men turned around and went back. When they arrived, they reported every word. David said to his men, "Put on your swords!" So they put on their swords, and David put on his. About four hundred men went up with David, while two hundred stayed with the supplies.*
>
> —1 Samuel 25:10-13

The first words out of Nabal's mouth highlight the writer's description of this foolish man as "surly and mean in his dealings." There's little reason to think that a shrewd businessman like Nabal wouldn't have heard of David. In fact, David's original message had no mention of Jesse, and yet Nabal knows who the fugitive's father is. Perhaps Nabal's veiled insult of David's purported anonymity was energized by Samuel's recent death "which was mourned by all of Israel"—including Nabal's household, to be sure. Everybody knew that Saul was out to get David, and Samuel wasn't around to stand up for the fugitive, *so why not*, Nabal thinks, *just have a little fun with the vagabond and tell him to go take a hike*.

It's hard to understand the motivation of people who are constantly mean-spirited like Nabal. A contemporary example might be found in the story of Ty Cobb, once called "the most-hated man in baseball." His parents named him after the tumultuous Lebanon city of Tyre. Though an exceptionally-talented player (no one has ever beaten his lifetime batting average of .366), he was perpetually saying and doing things to alienate his teammates, coaches, the media, and even the fans. According to one of his biographers, he died alone, clutching a gun and millions of dollars to his chest.

It's unusual, but there really are people out there who feel alive only when they're making people angry. Perpetual conflict is the only thing that energizes them, and to resolve problems with people (with whom they continually stir up resentment) only diminishes their sense of well-being. It's reasonable to assume that Nabal was a man driven by a similar internal engine.

A Call to Arms

Apparently surprised by Nabal's insolence, David called his men to arms. They had reported every word to David—you can almost picture him biting his lower lip as Nabal snobbishly puts down David's purported reputation as a fierce fighter. The spirit of Nabal's words said this: *This David, whoever he is, is probably nothing more than a wounded puppy running from the rolled up newspaper of an annoyed owner.* These words, which Nabal probably knew would be conveyed verbatim, were clearly intended to chafe and insult David. But, based on Nabal's later response to the news that David was coming, the wealthy rancher probably did not expect the fugitive to do anything about it. In Nabal's mind, David was probably just another one of those overly-sensitive folks who seem to cross Nabal's path all the time.

David had originally sent ten unarmed men with a reasonable request. Now he was going to send 400 seasoned warriors with swords so sharp they could slice through the leather breastplate of a common bodyguard as easily as a box cutter goes through cardboard. No niceties or small talk this time — no negotiations either. The writer makes it clear that David also armed himself, so there was going to be no "watching the battle from a hilltop" for this future commander-in-chief of Israel.

Consider what is probably going on in David's mind at this time. He's surrounded by 600 hungry men who are putting their lives on the line to protect the future king. Keep in mind that Saul is still out in the wilderness with 3000 men trying to hunt down his successor—and anyone with David who is showing even the slightest bit of support to the fugitive. Look at what happened to the priests of Ahimelech, who just gave David a little bread (1 Sam. 21-22). Saul had them all killed by the only one of his officers who was willing to murder these innocent men. It's quite possible that Nabal heard about the slaughter of these priests by the hand of Saul and lacked the courage to help the fugitive and his band. However, if there was any cowardice on Nabal's part, it was covered by his empty bravado.

Like many political supporters today, those who are closest to the candidate are often rewarded by positions of power within the new administration. It's likely that several of these men expected to be elevated in David's kingdom once he rose to power—and the longer they protected this future king, the likelihood of that happening only increased. As in all political campaigns, however, the perception of strength and resolve is all-important if the candidate wants to rise to power. And now, here in front of his men, is an insolent rancher telling David that he can just go pick berries off the desert bushes if he's hungry because he's too small in Nabal's eyes to even offer a crumb.

> *David had just said, "It's been useless—all my watching over this fellow's property in the desert so that nothing of his was missing. He has paid me back evil for good. May God deal with David, be it ever so severely, if by morning I leave alive one male of all who belong to him!"*
>
> *—1 Samuel 25:21-22*

Now that David's been challenged, he feels he has to make a strong, public display of how deeply offended he is—and clearly he has nothing to fake or exaggerate here. How would it look if the future king of Israel let such a vile insult pass—especially in the full view of hundreds of famished warriors looking for a fight? David invokes an oath and vows to slaughter every single male in Nabal's household—including Nabal, of course. Maybe David would save him for last. To this end, David gives the emotionally-charged order to fight. He is out for blood.

What's in a name?

> *One of the servants told Nabal's wife Abigail: "David sent messengers from the desert to give our master his greetings, but he hurled insults at them. Yet these men were very good to us. They did not mistreat us, and the whole time we were out in the fields near them nothing was missing. Night and day they were a wall around us all the time we were herding our sheep near them. Now think it over and see what you can do, because disaster is hanging over our master and his whole household.*

> He is such a wicked man that no one can talk to
> him."
> —1 Samuel 25:14-17

Sometimes people choose vocations that are a reflection of their names. One study discovered a Mr. Warmbath who was a hotel manager, a Mr. Barnacle who was a marine timber expert, a Dr. Grunt who specialized in animal behavior, and a Miss Beat, who was, of course, a music teacher.

Many Native American tribes give their young people names that reflect something that has been observed about them. If you've seen the movie, *Dances with Wolves*, you may remember "Stands with a Fist" and "Kicking Bird." If I had been born into a Native American tribe, they'd probably call me something like "Sits with a Book" or "Runs like a Fat Antelope."

There are several people in the Bible, who, unfortunately, were named after rather tragic events. There is Jabez, whose mother named him after her painful birthing experience bringing him into the world. There's Hosea's son, Jezreel, named after a famous massacre, and his daughters Lo-ruhamah, to call attention to Israel's alienation from God, and Lo-ammi, to remind God's people that He was fed up with them and no longer wanted anything to do with them.

Another biblical character with an unfortunate name was Nabal. His Hebrew name meant "fool." One has to wonder what his parents were thinking. Even so, as an adult, he wasted no time living up to his name. Though apparently a successful businessman, he had apparently alienated not only his workers, but also his wife and probably other members of his family. In today's corporate world, people like this often get deservedly tagged as "micro-managers" or "non-team players."

In the proverbs, Solomon had a lot to say about fools—what they were like and how to best deal with them. Let's take a look at these particular proverbs to get a better idea of what Nabal was really like.

> A fool shows his annoyance at once, but a
> prudent man overlooks an insult.
> —Proverbs 12:16

The fool has very little patience with those who will not conform to his immediate and inconsiderate desires. To the fool, a win-win solution means "do it my way (I win), and I won't make your life miserable (so you win too!)."

> It is to a man's honor to avoid strife, but every
> fool is quick to quarrel.
> —Proverbs 20:3

Fools love a fight; and they're often quite good at it. They are amazingly competent when it comes to using volume and intimidation (not necessarily logic or reasoning) to win an argument. At least they keep thinking that they're truly persuading their opponents, because most of the people who continually engage a fool soon weary of the unending struggle and just give in.

> Fools mock at making amends for sin, but good
> will is found among the upright.
> —Proverbs 14:9

Solomon's fool is the poster-child of the immovable and unrepentant. In the fool's mind, the people around him need to stop overreacting to his "reasonable" unilateral and non-reciprocating demands. Again, he cannot, or will not, internalize personal responsibility for his actions. His favorite retort usually goes something like, "If you hadn't [blank], then this [his failure] wouldn't have happened." He will usually focus on what was less-than-ideal about the rescuer's response to his irresponsible act— rather than on the act itself. Fools are masters of deflection.

> A fool gives full vent to his anger, but a wise
> man keeps himself under control.
> —Proverbs 29:11

Anger is the weapon of choice for the fool; he demands conformity to his opinions, values, and plans—and he'll use whatever wrathful energy he needs in order to insure compliance to his demands.

> The fear of the LORD is the beginning of knowl-
> edge, but fools despise wisdom and discipline.
> —Proverbs 1:7

For the fool, to learn something new is to concede that there's something he doesn't already know—and, in his mind, he's pretty close to being omniscient. If you attempt to present some sort of solution to him, he'll tell you that he thought about that a long time ago—and then give you several reasons why it would never work. Keep in mind, the fool does not like solutions—it's the continuing problem and ongoing conflict that keeps him energized.

> *The wise in heart accept commands, but a chattering fool comes to ruin.*
>
> —*Proverbs* 10:8

The fool is quick to give unsolicited advice in areas of life where he is clearly failing. Since he shuns responsibility for his own lack of success but projects that blame on to others, he sees no inconsistency with offering this type of expert advice.

> *The way of a fool seems right to him, but a wise man listens to advice.*
>
> —*Proverbs* 12:15

The fool will never, ever concede that he could possibly be wrong. If you disagree with him, then either you don't fully understand what he's trying to say (because you have an intelligence problem), or you're simply looking for a fight—which he's more than happy to perpetuate.

> *He who walks with the wise grows wise, but a companion of fools suffers harm.*
>
> —*Proverbs* 13:20

The seductive quality of many fools is that they seem to attract people who want to rescue them. The sensitive person thinks, "If I give in to what he wants, he'll be more reasonable." Of course the fool welcomes their company because most rescuers are easily exploited and manipulated. But in the end, only the self-appointed deliverer suffers—because the fool has no interest in being saved from anything.

> *As a dog returns to its vomit, so a fool repeats his folly.*
>
> —*Proverbs* 26:11

This rather graphic analogy captures the essence of why fools keep repeating the same destructive behaviors. Since they shun all sense of personal responsibility, the reasons for their repetitive actions rest outside of them—and so, therefore, must the solution. They say "if so-and-so would just [blank], then this wouldn't keep happening." So they keep repeating the same harmful actions over and over again—and blaming others for the same damaging consequences that naturally keep occurring.

> *Though you grind a fool in a mortar, grinding him like grain with a pestle, you will not remove his folly from him.*
>
> *—Proverbs 27:22*

Fools cannot and will not change, at least not without intervention from God. And even then, God is not going to force them to change against their will. Trying to change a fool is like trying to dig a hole in the sidewalk with a plastic spoon—it just isn't going to happen.

Even the most compassionate of the "rescuer-types" cannot change the heart of a foolish person. Acknowledging the damage they have caused is so repulsive to their deeply-ingrained blameshifting tendencies that it seems humanly impossible for them to ever repent—either in this life or the next.

> Evil is present when there is a profound absence of empathy, shame, and goodness. Empathy involves a connectedness to the heart of another and respect for their personal boundaries. An evil person is unmoved by the inner world of the other and has no respect for boundaries ... An evil person seems to delight in stripping away purpose, individuality, and vitality.
>
> Dan Allender in *Bold Love*

> *Abigail lost no time. She took two hundred loaves of bread, two skins of wine, five dressed sheep, five seahs of roasted grain, a hundred cakes of raisins and two hundred cakes of pressed figs, and loaded them on donkeys. Then she told her servants, "Go on ahead; I'll follow you." But she did not tell her husband Nabal.*
>
> *As she came riding her donkey into a mountain ravine, there were David and his men descending toward her, and she met them.*
>
> *—1 Samuel 25:18-20*

ENTER ABIGAIL, NABAL'S WIFE. A lot has been written about this woman—and not all of it very nice. She's been called a "doormat with lace," "a usurper of her husband's authority," and "a sneak who does things without her spouse's knowledge." The biblical writer, on the other hand, uses two words to describe Abigail—beautiful and intelligent—so her actions should only be interpreted in light of those descriptives (1 Sam. 25:3).

When Nabal stirs up trouble, which he's apparently prone to do, the servants know right where to go—straight to Abigail. As David expected, these servants vouched for the good behavior of the fugitive future-king and his men. We see here that David was doing more than just not harassing them—he was serving as a wall of protection for these herds and those who watched over them.

Apparently they didn't waste their time telling Nabal about David's angry response to the rancher's insults. Their lives were now on the line, and they knew that their master would only make the situation worse—for them and himself. This man was so focused on getting others to acknowledge that he was right, he could not analyze, much less listen to, any facts that contradicted his foregone conclusions. This man was so immovable in his opinions, that, according to his servants, "No one can talk to him."

Abigail acted immediately . . . and apparently she also knew better than to waste any time bringing the problem to Nabal. She gathered loads and loads of supplies and told her servants to take these to David and attempt to head him off at the pass.

Clearly, Abigail was as level-headed as Nabal was an idiot. First, she didn't expend any energy talking to a man whose very name meant "fool." It's simply impossible to negotiate with someone who always demands conformity to his or her ideas and values. You may spend all kinds of time, money, and other resources attempting to compromise with such an individual—but in the end, you always end up back at square one . . . which is nothing less, or nothing more, than what the foolish person angrily demanded in the first place.

Secondly, Abigail came after, not before, all the supplies she had prepared for David and his men. (I'm sure she didn't even give a second thought about attempting to meet the angry fugitive without such a gift). Jacob did something similar when he was preparing to meet a potentially-hostile visitor—his brother Esau, of whom he ripped off the birthright for a bowl of stew (Gen. 32). Jacob sent loads and loads of gifts ahead of him in the hopes of pacifying his fiery brother before he actually came face-to-face with him. Known for his cunning ways, this was a shrewd act of self-preservation on Jacob's part.

Excluding the craftiness, Abigail probably had the same thing in mind when she sent all these supplies ahead of her. Not only was she meeting a reasonable and intense material need (hunger), she was giving David a chance to save face in front of his men—should he choose to pull back from his intended attack. Perhaps as a sign of her peaceful intentions and humble attitude, she approached David riding on a donkey and put herself in the extremely vulnerable position of being descended upon in a ravine.

> When Abigail saw David, she quickly got off her donkey and bowed down before David with her face to the ground. She fell at his feet and said: "My lord, let the blame be on me alone. Please let your servant speak to you; hear what your servant has to say. May my lord pay no attention to that wicked man Nabal. He is just like his name—his name is Fool, and folly goes with him. But as for me, your servant, I did not see the men my master sent.
>
> "Now since the LORD has kept you, my master, from bloodshed and from avenging yourself with your own hands, as surely as the LORD lives and as you live, may your enemies and all who intend to harm my master be like Nabal. And let this gift, which your servant has brought to my master, be given to the men who follow you. Please forgive your servant's offense, for the LORD will certainly make a lasting dynasty for my master, because he fights the LORD's battles. Let no wrongdoing be found in you as long as you live. Even though someone is pursuing you to take your life, the life of my master will be bound securely in the bundle of the living by the LORD your God. But the lives of your enemies he will hurl away as from the pocket of a sling. When the LORD has done for my master every good thing he promised concerning him and has appointed him

> *leader over Israel, my master will not have on his*
> *conscience the staggering burden of needless blood-*
> *shed or of having avenged himself. And when the*
> *LORD has brought my master success, remember*
> *your servant."*
>
> —*1 Samuel 25:23-31*

To her already-vulnerable position, Abigail falls on her face before the would-be avenger who already had his hand on the hilt of his sword. Surely, to the words *beautiful* and *intelligent*, we can add the word *courageous* to Abigail's character traits.

The second thing Abigail did to assuage David's anger (the first being the gift of food) was to take full responsibility for the crisis. Nothing arrests the anger of a person in power quicker than someone taking responsibility for an unfortunate situation. As a manager, I don't like to hear bad news, but I want to be told as soon as some sort of crisis occurs. Nothing clarifies my thinking, however, more than for a trusted and loyal employee to tell me in such a situation, "A terrible thing has happened and it's my fault. I'm responsible for what happened." There's no finger-pointing, blameshifting, or responsibility-dodging on the part of the employee. With that out of the way, we can deal directly with the problem and think of ways to prevent it from happening in the future. In addition, his self-effacing acknowledgment compels me to examine my contribution to the crisis as the supervisor. And my confidence in that team member only increases because I know that in the future, he will take full responsibility for his work.

NOW THAT ABIGAIL HAS LOWERED DAVID'S DEFENSES and had his complete and undivided attention, she makes her request. She respectfully asks him to ignore the slights of an undisciplined and ignorant man—namely her foolish husband. For David to shed the blood of such an unworthy foe, especially a civilian, would only haunt him in the future. While no one would have blamed David for wiping out Nabal's community, Abigail knew that such an act would be considered an illegitimate act of revenge that God had strictly prohibited (Deut. 32:35; Lev. 19:18).

Clearly, Abigail knew that David had been appointed by God, and even though he was being hunted down by a declining tyrant, the Lord would one day elevate him to be king over Israel. Abigail speaks of herself in the third person, calling herself "servant" to David. Based on David's reputation as a godly man, she is confident that he will not abuse that power in her state of heightened vulnerability.

> David said to Abigail, "Praise be to the LORD,
> the God of Israel, who has sent you today to meet
> me. May you be blessed for your good judgment and
> for keeping me from bloodshed this day and from
> avenging myself with my own hands. Otherwise, as
> surely as the LORD, the God of Israel, lives, who has
> kept me from harming you, if you had not come
> quickly to meet me, not one male belonging to Nabal
> would have been left alive by daybreak."
>
> Then David accepted from her hand what she
> had brought him and said, "Go home in peace. I
> have heard your words and granted your request."
> —1 Samuel 25:32-35

David is so impressed by Abigail's humility and wisdom that he calls off the attack. She has given him an opportunity to save face in front of his men (who are now also amply supplied), and he accepts that gift from her hand. David does not hold back on telling her what would have happened. He wouldn't have hesitated to kill her either—but because of her good judgment, he stayed his hand and granted her request.

Now, maybe we know the rest of the story, but at this point David does not know what's going to happen. As far as he's concerned, this intelligent woman is going to go back to her arrogant husband, tell him what happened, and Nabal's going to laugh at David's apparent weakness. Nabal's going to sink even deeper into his sense of self-justification and David will have done nothing. David's men have been fed . . . but maybe he wondered "have I lost some of their respect?"

This is where the rubber meets the road when it comes to having an opportunity to take vengeance into your own hands and choosing to step aside and "leave room for the wrath of God." Once again, the repeat offender gets away with something and attributes it to his own brilliance—or perhaps, to your weakness. Will you still stay your hand? Because it's at this point where "trusting God" becomes more than Christian jargon and becomes the emotional energy by which you stop yourself from doing something you're only going to regret.

> When Abigail went to Nabal, he was in the house holding a banquet like that of a king. He was in high spirits and very drunk. So she told him nothing until daybreak. Then in the morning, when Nabal was sober, his wife told him all these things, and his heart failed him and he became like a stone. About ten days later, the LORD struck Nabal and he died.
> —1 Samuel 25:36-38

SO ABIGAIL DID GO BACK TO TELL NABAL WHAT HAPPENED but found that he had been partying and was totally inebriated. If there's anything worse than talking with a fool, it's talking with a drunken fool. So she decides to hold off until he sobers up. The fact that Nabal is holding such a banquet, even as four hundred men are roaring down the hill to mow him down along with his guests, only highlights his ignorance, insolence, and arrogance.

Instead of laughing at Abigail's account of everything that happened, as we might expect, Nabal suddenly realized the terrible fate he just barely escaped. It would have been bad enough to be sober and meet such a furious foe, but he and his body guards were probably too drunk to even lift their swords, much less defend themselves. Instead of regret, however, it's quite possible that he was so angry about his heightened assailability (which of course, in his mind, was the fault of his wife and servants), that he might have had a stroke. The biblical description of him becoming "like a stone" seems to support the idea of some sort of aneurysm—which, in this culture, could legitimately be called heart failure.

Ten days later, the foolish man died.

> *When David heard that Nabal was dead, he said, "Praise be to the LORD, who has upheld my cause against Nabal for treating me with contempt. He has kept his servant from doing wrong and has brought Nabal's wrongdoing down on his own head."*
>
> *Then David sent word to Abigail, asking her to become his wife. His servants went to Carmel and said to Abigail, "David has sent us to you to take you to become his wife."*
>
> *She bowed down with her face to the ground and said, "Here is your maidservant, ready to serve you and wash the feet of my master's servants."*
>
> *Abigail quickly got on a donkey and, attended by her five maids, went with David's messengers and became his wife.*
>
> —1 Samuel 25:39-42

When David gets the news that the man he came very close to killing in a vengeful rage was now dead by the Lord's hand and not his own, the future king praised God for the act of vindication. And on top of the vindication, David proposes marriage to the fool's widow—which she accepts in the same humble manner in which she approached him during their first encounter.

We can be confident that this miraculous intervention by God did more to shape the way David dealt with his enemies than any other preinaugural experience—perhaps even more than being chased by Saul in the wilderness and deciding NOT, on two occasions, to take the life of his mad pursuer.

To be sure, David later became known as a fierce warrior—so much so, that God did not want him to build the temple because of his reputation for being a man of blood. However, all of these exploits were military in nature. Of course, David had Uriah killed to cover up the king's grossly immoral act—but he did not do this as a vendetta. As far as we know, David never attacked anyone in an act of personal vengeance—though he came very close to doing so here.

It's important to keep this restrained public behavior in mind when we look at David's response to this type of evil in his private prayers.

WHEN I WAS IN MIDDLE SCHOOL, I loved to read those Christian cartoon tracts where the "sinners" always had dark circles under their eyes, and the "saved" always looked like they had just gotten up from a refreshing two-hour nap. There was a heavy emphasis on God's judgment in these tracts, and the publishers would often portray the "sinners" and "saved" as standing before the judgment throne of God.

The "sinners" in these tracts often expressed regret that they didn't repent during their earthly lives. But now that they had seen, face-to-face, the God they had rejected all their lives, it was too late. They wanted to repent, but the option was no longer available.

The Bible's portrayal of the unrepentant who stand before God seems to go against the grain of these cartoon tracts. According to the Scriptures, Satan was once a magnificent creature who held great authority in the presence of God. After he rebelled, he apparently continued to appear before the throne of God, presumably to boast against and provoke the Lord. There is no greater portrayal of the devil's arrogance in this regard than when he's attempting to bait God into testing the integrity of Job's faith (Job 1). In this encounter, he certainly gives no indication of ever repenting—even though he can see the Lord in all of his glory.

The doomed wealthy man in Jesus' story of the rich man and Lazarus, also seems to show no desire to repent—he simply wants a bit more physical comfort in his torment. Like the earthly fool, he continues to display no sense of personal responsibility. He thinks someone rising from the dead might convince his brothers to repent, but he shows no such interest for himself. In the story, Abraham laments that even if someone were to be raised from the dead, they would still not repent. [Ironically, here is Abraham and Lazarus—both raised from the dead and standing in front of this man—and he still shows no regrets, other than his discomfort.]

Another set of unrepentant folks who appear before God on the Day of Judgment are the "goats"—whom Jesus separates from the "sheep" (Matt. 25:31-46). The "goats" dare to argue with Jesus about when it was they were supposed to have seen Him in need and didn't help him.

[It's interesting to note that the wording of the "sheep's" response in this story is similar to that of the "goats" except that the sheep repeat the actions that Jesus described, and the goats do not—because the goats know they didn't do any of these things for anyone, much less Jesus.]

AS HARD AS IT MIGHT BE TO UNDERSTAND, there are people in the world who will forever and always be permanently remorseless. And if God will not compel them to feel contrition, certainly we will never be able to do so. While we're commanded to offer them the opportunity to repent (as we will talk about later), the decision to acknowledge what they have done must come from within.

Consequently, we must never allow our emotional health, which depends on our ability to forgive someone, to remain wholly dependent on that person's willingness to bear the burden of what he or she has done — because it very well may never, ever happen.

While we must take the unchanging nature of the unrepentant fool quite seriously, of course, we must never label someone as beyond redemption. We simply don't have to the tools to accurately determine such an irreversible state, no matter what our brains and experience might be telling us. Our obligation is to safely and responsibly offer these people the opportunity to acknowledge what they've done—and some do respond positively. Sometimes it takes as long for people to genuinely repent as it does for the targets of their cruelty to forgive them.

If a former fool genuinely repents—that is, he fully acknowledges his sin, the damage that he caused, and attempts to replace his former bad behavior with actions that honor the Lord—he becomes an absolutely unstoppable force for the kingdom of God. As Jesus reminded his disciples, in essence, he who is forgiven much, loves much (Luke 7:47). But, again, the healing process cannot wait—you must move forward regardless of how they respond to you.

I'M GUESSING THAT THE STORY OF NABAL, ABIGAIL, AND DAVID is a favorite Bible story of intelligent and courageous women who are married to fools like Nabal. The bad guy is taken out of the picture—by the hand of God. And not just a prince, but a future *king* arrives on his noble steed, right behind the pallbearers, ready to sweep the wise and sensitive widow off her feet.

But sometimes the fool doesn't go away. In fact, he becomes more insolent and only increases in his arrogance. While he's not doing anything that would get him arrested, he perpetuates an atmosphere where everyone seems to be suffocating. The hapless spouse cleans up mess, after mess, after mess—trying to salvage her household. The white knight never comes to put the fool in his place, no one is rescued, resources are diminishing, and personal vindication seems like nothing more than a pipe dream.

What would you do then?

2 To Forgive
or
Not to Forgive

Even though full reconciliation with the remorseless may be impossible—much less appropriate—finding the ability to forgive these unrepentant offenders is physically, emotionally, and spiritually the healthiest thing to do.

Is "refusing to forgive" even an option for Christians? There are many powerful voices in the church who would say "No." According to these respected people, you must find some way to forgive.

Consider the unyielding words of C. S. Lewis on this topic:

> "To forgive the incessant provocations of the daily life—to keep on forgiving the bossy mother-in-law, the bullying husband, the nagging wife, the selfish daughter, the deceitful son—how can we do it? Only, I think, by remembering where we stand, by meaning our words when we say in our prayers each night 'Forgive us our trespasses as we forgive those who trespass against us.' We are offered forgiveness on no other terms. To refuse it is to refuse God's mercy for ourselves. There is no hint of exceptions, and God means what He says."

If, by chance his readers missed the point, Lewis put it in even simpler terms:

> *"We must forgive all our enemies or be damned."*

ONE MORNING I OPENED THE NEWSPAPER and read the headline, "I Will Never Forgive You."

The article began with these words: "For the second time, prosecutors failed to get a first-degree murder conviction in the death of a teen-age boy when a jury on Friday found the defendant guilty of one count of accessory to murder . . . coupled with an earlier jury decision that the defendant's accomplice was also an accessory in the slaying, the resulting verdict is a paradox: no one has been convicted of pulling the trigger of the shotgun that fatally wounded a young man on Valentine's Day."

As only an accessory to murder, the defendant could get as little as a three-year sentence. Since he had already been in jail two years awaiting trial, he could be out in less than a year. The father of the victims addressed one of the defendants after the trial. "You gave me and my family a life sentence . . . I will never forgive you."

For all its obvious benefits, sometimes forgiveness can seem like an emotionally-insurmountable task. Some psychologists even suggest, in certain cases, that you shouldn't even try.

It's tempting to think that we can gain something by not forgiving someone who has absolutely no interest in being reconciled with us—at least on appropriate terms. First, we assume that they're going to care about our withheld forgiveness, but you're probably just projecting your own sensitivities onto someone who might best be described as having no conscience. It's like trying to project an image onto a piece of glass—the image simply passes through and has little, if no, visual effect. The fact that you're withholding forgiveness in order to punish them is, to them, quite laughable.

Some think they'll lose their sense of self-respect if they forgive. We're assuming here that the established systems of justice have run their course, and as far as the offender is concerned the whole experience has been little more than a slap on the wrist. He might even be daring you to forgive him so his sense of "getting away with it" will be even greater. Forgiving someone under these circumstances appears to only add insult to injury. Our inability, or unwillingness, to forgive—in these circumstances—is directly related to a low-level of confidence that God will one day have the final word on the person's harmful behavior.

My sister and I grew up in a rather hostile home because our mom was a manic depressive. While I would never call our mom evil, her illness had many evil manifestations—nothing illegal, but certainly words and actions that we would call "boundary-violating" behaviors. Because she would fluctuate between a blue funk and focused rage, we were constantly walking on eggshells around her. But God, in His graciousness, brought a few loving mothers into our lives (all with their own families) to fill in the gaps that our mom's illness had created. Even after Mom passed away, they were still there. These days our step-mom and respective mother-in-laws continue to fill those empty spaces.

Some of these women, who had experienced no little pain in their own lives, seemed to have a singular message for us: *Never allow your suffering to generate a long-lasting sense of entitlement in your heart.* Sure, it's okay to feel sorry for yourself for a little while, perhaps to retreat and regroup so you can get a perspective on things. But once the healing begins, abandon these temporary respites and focus your renewed energy on other healthy relationships and endeavors. If you don't, you will become like those who have hurt you, because many of them are acting upon a well-entrenched (but false) sense of entitlement.

Entering into the process of forgiveness necessarily means that we have to let go of any entitling "self-talk" that might have developed as a coping mechanism. Some justify blatant sin in their lives just because they have suffered. For example, they might say to themselves, even unconsciously, "I have been hurt deeply, so it's okay for me to be rude, or to lie, or to exploit others—because if I don't, they're certainly going to take advantage of me." And this proves to be another reason why people don't want to consider forgiveness. It means they'll have to abandon the false comfort that the words have brought to them for so long—*"Since I've been ripped off, I have don't have to play by the rules."*

Probably the biggest reason people choose not to explore the process of forgiveness is something we'll call "The Jonah Syndrome." As you may recall from the story of Jonah, the reluctant prophet ran in the opposite direction when he was told by God to offer repentance to one of the fiercest superpowers the world has ever known—the Assyrians, specifically the inhabitants of the capital of the empire, Ninevah.

Sometimes, when a city was about to come under siege by the Assyrians, the citizens would simply kill each other rather than face the vicious, blood-curdling torture of these particular warriors. These mercenaries implemented methods of anguish that would maximize and draw out a person's pain experience without actually killing him. When the Assyrians captured their enemies, especially rival kings, they gouged their eyes out, and/or cut off their hands and feet, and/or staked them to the desert floor and skinned them alive—or, barring all this, slowly boiled or roasted them over a period of days.

No wonder Jonah was reluctant to pay these folks a visit.

The Scriptures are not clear why Jonah ran away from God's command to preach to these people. Many assume he was afraid—and there's certainly enough cultural evidence to back up that assertion. But looking at Jonah's angry response when these mercenaries did repent seems to indicate that he didn't want to confront these people because they might actually acknowledge their sin. These cruel, vicious, heartless people might actually take responsibility for what they were doing and never face the full wrath of God for their actions. When they actually did repent, Jonah was furious.

Genuine repentance is a form of justice that is eternally satisfactory in the eyes of God—because it ultimately draws upon the crucifixion of Christ for its basis and justification. And the crucifixion of Jesus was an historical event of such physical, emotional, and spiritual magnitude that it made the Assyrian torture experience look like a pat on the back.

Many reformed theologians would assert that God is equally glorified by total and defiant rejection of His grace as He is by the genuine repentance of the broken-hearted sinner. Even so, we are to desire and pursue the penance of our offenders. To those in our immediate circle who have hurt us, we are compelled to also offer them an opportunity to repent. We are to do this no matter how repelled we might be by the prospect that they might turn toward God and be forgiven the temporal and eternal consequences of their sins against us. If we don't, God is sure to creatively remind us, as He did with Jonah, that his concern for the evil and foolish people of this world is immeasurable—even though, in some cases, that is humanly incomprehensible.

The maintenance energy for withholding forgiveness is enormous. We might discreetly keep our ears open for bad news about these people so we can do a little fist-pumping as we rejoice in their misfortune. But, if we're in this state, hearing about their good fortune only plunges us into greater despair. The evil act might find its way into conversations that have nothing to do with the person we're talking to or the topic at hand. And, at the very worst, the harm we want to do to the offender, and can't, gets projected onto those who really do care about us. So our other relationships suffer because we can't find the ability to forgive.

Despite the difficulty of forgiving under certain circumstances, believers are often encouraged to forgive—no matter what. One simply has to read the words of C. S. Lewis quotes in the beginning of this chapter to understand what many believers feel is at stake if we don't forgive others "from the heart."

Lewis came to these conclusions, in part, from his understanding of Jesus' terrifying Parable of the Unmerciful Servant.

> *Then Peter came to Jesus and asked, "Lord, how many times shall I forgive my brother when he sins against me? Up to seven times?"*
>
> *Jesus answered, "I tell you, not seven times, but seventy-seven times.*
>
> *"Therefore, the kingdom of heaven is like a king who wanted to settle accounts with his servants. As he began the settlement, a man who owed him ten thousand talents was brought to him. Since he was not able to pay, the master ordered that he and his wife and his children and all that he had be sold to repay the debt.*
>
> *"The servant fell on his knees before him. 'Be patient with me,' he begged, 'and I will pay back everything.' The servant's master took pity on him, canceled the debt and let him go.*
>
> *"But when that servant went out, he found one of his fellow servants who owed him a hundred denarii. He grabbed him and began to choke him. 'Pay back what you owe me!' he demanded.*

"His fellow servant fell to his knees and begged him, 'Be patient with me, and I will pay you back.'

"But he refused. Instead, he went off and had the man thrown into prison until he could pay the debt. When the other servants saw what had happened, they were greatly distressed and went and told their master everything that had happened.

"Then the master called the servant in. 'You wicked servant,' he said, 'I canceled all that debt of yours because you begged me to. Shouldn't you have had mercy on your fellow servant just as I had on you?' In anger his master turned him over to the jailers to be tortured, until he should pay back all he owed.

"This is how my heavenly Father will treat each of you unless you forgive your brother from your heart."

—Matthew 18:21-35

Early in this same Gospel, Jesus said to his disciples,

"If you do not forgive men their sins, your Father will not forgive your sins."

—Matthew 6:15

The "If They Repent/Don't Repent" Question . . .

Ah, some have argued . . . there's a loophole here. We are to forgive those who offend us—but only if they repent. Consider Jesus' qualifiers in the Gospel of Luke:

"If your brother sins, rebuke him, and if he repents, forgive him."

—Luke 17:3

"If he sins against you seven times in a day, and seven times comes back to you and says, 'I repent,' forgive him."

—Luke 17:4

And in the same chapter where Jesus tells the parable of the forgiving and then unforgiving taskmaster (Matt. 18:21-35), He outlines the process of confronting the impenitent wrongdoing of someone in the church. If the offender refuses to acknowledge his sin, after several offers to repent by a variety of mature people who have established the facts in the matter, then he is to be treated as an unbeliever and expelled from the congregation. Even the Apostle Paul said, "Warn a divisive person once, then warn him a second time. After that, have nothing to do with him" (Titus 3:10).

Where is the forgiveness in that? Where then, is the balance? It seems odd for the Christian to say "No, I haven't forgiven that person—and I'm not sure if I'm ever going to."

Since the question of forgiveness seems to hinge upon the nature of true repentance, perhaps it would serve us well to see what true and false repentance is really like.

While you may find several people in the Bible asking God to forgive someone else, you'd be hard pressed to find many people in the Bible actually saying "Forgive me." (David says it sincerely only twice in the Psalms, Pharaoh and Saul say it insincerely, and Paul says it sarcastically in 2 Cor. 12:13.)

What you do find genuinely repentant people in the Bible doing is acknowledging and "owning" the wrongs that they have committed, and then, in response to this admission, receiving God's forgiveness and the forgiveness of others—usually without the offender ever asking for it.

The old definition of *repentance*—the one that says this word means to "turn around" or to "change one's mind" (while accurate as literal translations)—in our day has been reduced to something you can do over a decaf latte and a lemon bar.

What does the real thing look like?

If someone has hurt you and then expressed the desire to be fully restored in his or her relationship with you—what would you want from that person? What are the things that he or she would have to say and do in order for you to trust that person again?

The answer will give you a hint about what true repentance really is.

You would require nothing less than a full, detailed acknowledgment of the hurtful things he or she did to you, and then the full acceptance of responsibility for the resulting fallout of his or her actions—including all the pain you experienced. Along with this, you'd want to see that person attempting to correct the bad behavior by replacing it with something that's positively meaningful to you. And if the person failed in any of these, to ask for mercy.

In contrast, have you ever had the experience of being shafted by someone, and later he said something like "Oh, just forgive me for whatever it is I did that bothered you so much." If so, did that engender all kinds of warm feelings of reconciliation with that person? Probably not. What that person wanted was reconciliation without repentance.

Unfortunately, many people pursue a relationship with God in just the same way.

Repentance is more than just admitting you're a sinner. Even Pharaoh admitted he was a sinner (Exod. 9:27)—so did Balaam, Saul, and Judas (Num. 22:34; 1 Sam. 15:24; Matt. 27:4). But the consequential actions of these men illustrate that their admissions were little more than attempts to stall for more time, providing no evidence of soul-changing behavior.

True repentance is the hold-nothing-back acknowledgment of the wrong that has been done, including the damage it has caused, and the attempt to correct or appropriately replace the behavior. It is the difference between saying "I'm not perfect, just forgiven," *and* "I exploited that person's vulnerability, and, in so doing, crushed her spirit. If she will let me, I am now going to do whatever it takes to regain her trust."

It's as easy to remember as **A, B, C, . . . and M**

A — acknowledge the wrong that's been committed, **B** — bear the burden for the damage that behavior caused, and **C** — correct the errant behavior by replacing it with actions that honor God and the person you sinned against. And failing in any of these things because of human inadequacy and weakness, to ask for **M** — mercy.

While **A** and **B** are certainly difficult, **C** (that is, correcting the bad behavior by replacing it with a healthy behavior) proves to be the longevity test of genuine contrition. This is what John the Baptist meant when he said, "Produce fruit in keeping with repentance" (Matt. 3:8; Luke 3:8).

True repentance is not always a deeply emotional experience.

Depending on the personality type, the full acknowledgment of specific sins—and the resulting damage they have caused—can be an intensely cognitive experience. But while it may not always produce tears and the beating of one's chest, it is, nonetheless, often one of the most gut-wrenching things a person can do. So consequently, many people often avoid taking this painful step.

And even when repentance is done "perfectly," there remains a lingering sense of inadequacy on the part of the truly penitent sinner. Perhaps the offender acknowledges, in detail, that he's done something wrong. While crucial to reconciliation, all he's done is concede to

In Matthew 12, Jesus offers a lesson about spiritual exorcism, but it also has implications for the wisdom of replacing base behaviors with virtuous ones.

> When an evil spirit comes out of a man, it goes
> through arid places seeking rest and does not find it.
> Then it says, "I will return to the house I left."
> When it arrives, it finds the house unoccupied,
> swept clean and put in order. Then it goes and
> takes with it seven other spirits more wicked than
> itself, and they go in and live there. And the final
> condition of that man is worse than the first.
> —Matthew 12:43-45

In this story, there is a man who is oppressed by an evil spirit. He is freed from this particular demon but leaves "the house unoccupied." In this context, the Holy Spirit did not take residence in this man's heart because he did complete the process of deliverance—that is, becoming reconciled with God and thus sealed by the Holy Spirit (Eph. 1:13). And so, the original wicked spirit brings seven of his cohorts, and the final condition of the man is worse than the first.

Ask any recovering addict—if he does not replace the addictive behavior with something that does not harm him, the addiction will return in a blaze of horrific glory—and become even harder to overcome. The same is true with any bad behavior, especially an habitual one. A healthy action must be substituted, or the final condition will be worse than the first.

something that's true, perhaps even painfully obvious. As he bears the burden of the damage he has caused, he realizes that the consequences of his actions are far greater than he could ever repair. As he attempts to correct and replace his immoral behavior, he comes face-to-face with his own human weakness. At this point, if he truly desires reconciliation, all he can do is ask for mercy. This is probably what happened to the tax collector when he cried out, "God, have mercy on me, a sinner" (Luke 18:13).

> *He who conceals his sins does not prosper, but*
> *whoever confesses and renounces them finds mercy.*
> —*Proverbs 28:13*

True repentance—true enough to restore a human relationship or one's relationship with God—again, can be one of the most difficult, embarrassing, and agonizing things a human being can do. We don't have to look any further than our own hearts to know that this is true. This is the narrow path and the straight way—and it is a very difficult road to tread. But in the end, there simply is no other way to accomplish full reconciliation with God and others.

FEW PEOPLE QUESTION THE LIFE-GIVING BENEFITS OF THOUGHT-FUL FORGIVENESS—even for the most heinous of crimes. Forgiveness allows the victim to move on with her life. She accepts the fact that she's done everything she safely can to confront her offender—and there's nothing more to do (morally and legally). Forgiveness releases her from dwelling on other people's actions and social systems that are outside of her control. Forgiveness prevents her from projecting any bitterness and unresolved anger onto otherwise-innocent people in her life. The immense amount of emotional energy that unforgiveness drains can now be directed toward more life-enhancing activities and relationships. The obsessing, the grudge-nursing, and the fantasies of human revenge are all over.

Forgiveness and reconciliation are not always synonymous

For the sake of our discussion here, however, we need to be careful *not* to equate forgiveness with reconciliation. Undoubtedly, the acknowledgment of destructive behaviors is necessary for the full restoration of a damaged relationship to occur. Certainly, this is true of our relationship with God—no one's getting into heaven without first owning up to the wrongs he or she has committed.

We should expect no less in our relationships with one another. There can never be true reconciliation without genuine repentance. Granted, many marriages, friendships, and parent-child relationships continue on even though many unresolved issues lie unattended and unaddressed. But none of these relationships could legitimately be called healthy.

Most people think that granting forgiveness is simply a blank check to allow the offender back into their lives simply to trample on their heart again. Nothing could be further from the truth. Granted, we want to always allow reconciliation to be a possibility—but only if there's full acknowledgment (by the offender) of the immoral behavior and the resulting damage it has caused. However, if denial remains king, then the door of reconciliation must remain chain-locked—even while we are moving toward forgiveness in the context of this diminishing relationship.

For this reason, it's not healthy to talk about forgiveness as merely "the emotional release" of the debt that the people have created in our lives. Instead, it is better to describe forgiveness as the "transfer" of that debt from our account to God's. Forgiveness includes the acknowledgment that we are powerless to collect on certain debts and that we must trust God to balance the books. This is what God means when He promises "I will repay" (Deut. 32:35; Jer. 16:18; 25:14; 51:24; Ezek. 7:9; Joel 2:25; Rom. 12:19; Heb. 10:30; Rev. 2:23—Note, that in some of these passages, God's repayment plan also includes compensation to the victims).

Thus freed from this treadmill of futile liability collection, we are better able to offer our offenders the opportunity to repent instead of retaliating, to leave the door open for reconciliation, to publicly bless them (when appropriate), and to responsibly determine our future levels of vulnerability to them—all the while, "leaving room for God's wrath" (See Rom. 12:17-21—note the actions we are to take in this passage while still expecting God's disciplinary action against our offenders).

Forgiveness, when it is done well, is always a unilateral action— we should be moving in the direction of forgiveness *regardless* of the person's response to responsible confrontation.

However, the relational proximity of that person to us is *entirely* dependent on his or her response. If the person is moving toward genuine repentance, then perhaps full reconciliation is a possibility. However, if he or she is moving toward dismissal and blameshifting, then we should keep that person at a safe and perhaps ever-increasing distance.

The appropriate response to abused vulnerability is decreasing that vulnerability—or perhaps removing it all together. But don't throw the baby out with the bathwater and say you'll never make yourself vulnerable in any other safe, appropriate relationship. True intimacy is impossible without vulnerability.

The relationship of human beings with God can be described in this manner—they are either moving toward Him in a spirit of contrition and humility, or moving away from Him in a spirit of self-justification.

In this regard, there's just no standing still.

David's stumbling forgiveness

Let's fast-forward in David's life, to the middle of his reign, to see how he addressed the "to forgive or not to forgive question." In this dark period of his life, he found himself doing the "forgiveness thing" very poorly and thus needed to respond to one of the most personally evil and offensive acts against him—by someone in his own family.

David was an exceptionally-sharp national leader. He waged just war, formed alliances, and turned Israel into the superpower of the Mediterranean world. Israel's wealth and power during this period only grew under David's leadership—along with the unfortunate pressure of many outside enemies wanting a piece of that wealth, power, and militarily strategic land that Israel occupied.

The constant struggle of ancient rulers to defend their power and wealth is captured in the story commonly known as Damocles' Sword.

Dionysius, a 4th-century contemporary of Plato, was known as a cruel and vicious tyrant of the city of Syracuse, located on the eastern coast of modern-day Sicily. [Plato was known to visit Syracuse during the reign of Dionysius, so the tyrant and philosopher might have even had a conversation or two.]

Whoever controlled Syracuse controlled most of the island country—and Dionysius did so with an iron fist. Under Dionysius' rule, the city became one of the most glorious and well-fortified centers of commerce in the Greek empire—due mostly to his powerful Mediterranean navy.

Of course, Dionysius was constantly battling enemies who wanted his city and all the power that went with it. This was especially true of the Carthaginians to the west, who were pushed by Dionysius to the western part of (what is now) Sicily.

[According to Solomon, David also faced similar conditions of constant warfare and defense because of Israel's corridor location along the eastern coast of the Mediterranean. Israel did not know any significant peace until Solomon ascended to the throne.]

While ruthless and effective, Dionysius bore the constant burden of hundreds of people striving, struggling, and battling to obtain the riches, luxuries, and servants that only a man in his position of power could afford.

Dionysius was often visited by a rather servile man called Damocles, who was constantly commenting on how much fulfillment and satisfaction the tyrant must gain from holding on to such wealth and power. Dionysius eventually grew weary of this man's empty flattery, so he made Damocles an offer. Without officially giving up his power, he would allow Damocles—on the next day—to fully experience what it meant to be ruler over such a vast domain. Of course, Damocles would not refuse, and so he greedily anticipated what would happen on the following day.

When Damocles entered the courtroom the next morning, he was overwhelmed by the luxurious preparations that the tyrant had made for him. Servants doted on him hand and foot. They gave him a beautiful robe, and led him to a banquet table lavished with delicacies from all over the Mediterranean.

As Damocles was gorging himself at the table, he happened to look up. There, hanging from the ceiling and directly above his head, was a massive sword suspended by a mere horse's hair. Of course, upon seeing this, Damocles froze. The slightest movement could send the blade down upon him like a guillotine—and he would be gone forever. Surely, Dionysius was living up to his reputation as a tyrant by setting this trap.

Moved by Damocles' ghostly-pale appearance, he inquired as to what was the matter. "You dare ask what's wrong? I have this deadly sword hanging over my head, ready to take my life from me in an instant."

"Ah, so now you have gotten your wish," said the shrewd Dionysius. "Now you know what it's like to be ruler over such a powerful domain. True enough, I am surrounded by wealth, servants, and luxuries, but I cannot fully enjoy them. I spend my days underneath such a sword—battling enemies, subtle and overt—all of who would take my life in a second if doing so guaranteed that their position would be elevated—even in the slightest."

"I have learned my lesson," gulped Damocles, "I want nothing to do with your position, wealth, and power if it means living under this constant threat."

Any person in power—whether they are ancient kings or modern-day executives—live under Damocles' sword. No matter how much power you have, there will always be someone—or usually several people—waiting in the wings to wrest some or all of that power from you. While, of course, it's possible to be a good and effective leader even under this kind of pressure (in fact, it's a great test of leadership to honorably overcome these types of obstacles), it's easy to see how this form of stress could, over time, create an overwhelming sense of paranoia in a weak leader.

This was certainly true of Saul—this constant pressure was the very thing that drove him into the desert to chase after David—even while the rest of his kingdom was falling apart. All of history's tyrants—Nero, Hitler, Stalin, Idi Amin, and others like them, were driven to treachery and murder by this same overwhelming paranoia. Their fears were often backed up by strong empirical evidence—there were often several greedy people in their empires preparing for a coup.

We are told by Solomon that his father constantly faced warfare from all sides—externally and internally—throughout his reign (1 Kings 5:3). But David was an excellent administrator, and he surrounded himself with sharp people like his commander Joab and the prophet Nathan to keep him attentive and accountable.

But if David had an Achilles' heel, it was his lack of passion for being an active and involved father. While David was often furious about his children's misbehavior, he seldom—if ever—took corrective action with them.

Many commentators have given David low marks in the fathering column, and rightly so. Several of them blame Jesse's apparent disinterest in David. But I believe David's parenting troubles were due largely to his multiple marriages. David had to interact with several sons and daughters, all from different women. Moses made it clear that future kings were not to multiply wives unto themselves (Deut. 17:17). But for political and perhaps distorted virile reasons, the kings of Israel tended to ignore this command.

Not only kings, but even the patriarchs and other leaders seemed to have more than one wife. Really, what were these men thinking? While there seems to be several examples of polygamy in the Bible, there is not a single, successful example in the bunch. There is always strife between the wives (or the wives and concubines)—and the resultant offspring often seem to be at each other's throats. It's possible to trace the current tensions in the Middle East to this kind of ancient sibling rivalry.

Sometimes we see a contemporary example of this dynamic in the aftermath of remarriage after divorce. A man has children by his first wife, divorces, remarries, and then "adopts" the kids from wife #2. What often happens in these cases (but not all, of course), is that the man's world is suddenly split into seemingly-divergent universes. His biological children may vie for his attention. But he tells them, in one way or the other, that the group of people associated with his second marriage . . . well . . . they are his family now. And perhaps the adopted children from his second marriage long for their biological father. So entering into their world takes enormous emotional energy, so he tends to put them off as well. When the inevitable crisis rears its head—he'll push it onto the respective mother to deal with it and simply retreat further into his cave. And then, if the man also has children by his second wife, the situation becomes even more complex and difficult to handle. I'm certain that David was affected by this internal dynamic, and it caused him no end of strife and problems within his family.

Because of this major parenting tension in the life of this otherwise godly man, David came very close to losing his kingdom by the hand of his own son, Absalom. The first mention of Absalom as an adult is 2 Samuel 13—in the context of the violation of Absalom's sister, Tamar, by his half-brother, Amnon. When Amnon was finished with his despicable deed, the Scriptures say that he immediately hated Tamar even more than he thought he loved her. His reaction shows that these types of assaults have nothing to do with misguided affection, a longing for intimacy, or supposed-provocation—they are hate crimes of the worst kind.

When Absalom heard about his step-brother's lack of moral restraint and compassion, he took his sister in—and immediately started forming a plan for revenge that would take two years to implement. All this time, Absalom didn't say anything to Amnon that would have raised any suspicions.

In contrast, when David had heard what happened, he was livid—probably because he had been sucked in as unwilling participant in this deceptive ruse (Amnon had asked David to send Tamar to be his chef and nurse—and so David sent for her). But typical of David, the father, he did nothing to discipline Amnon. For such a vile act, Amnon should have been imprisoned, exiled, or perhaps even executed after all the indisputable facts of Amnon's guilt had been established in the king's court. But David just got irritated, and apparently let Amnon go about his business without any sort of accountability. The absence of any even-attempted justice probably infuriated the young Absalom all the more.

Twenty-four months later, Absalom set up a trap for Amnon at the time of sheepshearing—which was often a festive time. As you may recall, David's near-bloody encounter with Nabal happened at a similar time in the rancher's calendar. Ironically, David is unwittingly used again to set up an act of treachery. Absalom literally begs David to send Amnon to the wooly harvest. Reluctantly, David sends Amnon with the rest of his sons. Apparently, these were the last words that David and Absalom exchanged with one another for the next five years.

After getting Amnon drunk, Absalom ordered his men to strike him down. When the rest of the king's sons saw what happened, they all jumped on their horses and fled. At first, David received an inaccurate report that Absalom had, in fact, killed all of his sons. But David's nephew, Jonadab (who, ironically, gave Amnon the plan for cornering Tamar), told the king that only Amnon was dead.

In the meantime, Absalom fled into the wilderness to begin the exile from his father's kingdom. Absalom knew that David had little tolerance for blood spilled out of revenge—and so banishment was assured.

David was torn. He longed for his son, but he could not publicly allow such a deceptive avenger back into his kingdom. Joab, his loyal commander, had similarly killed a man who was vying for David's throne, and the king made a very public display of dissociating himself from this act of political assassination. Eventually, through the cunning story of Joab, (spoken through the lips of a widow), Absalom was allowed back into Jerusalem. But even then, he did not see his father for another two years. The cause of the estrangement was never addressed, even indirectly. Here we see "the process of forgiveness" entered into and drawn out very poorly.

> *"It should not be assumed that because a person*
> *has a theological understanding of forgiveness that*
> *he or she understands and practices interpersonal*
> *forgiveness."*
> —*Dr. Preston Van Loon*

Of course, Absalom was known for taking years to build a grudge, and he obviously resented David. He felt this way, not only because of his father's failure to bring Tamar's rapist to justice, but for exiling Absalom when the young man decided to take justice into his own hands. A shrewd and handsome man, Absalom began to win the hearts of the Israelites over to his side over the course of four years. And just as according to plan, when Absalom had sufficient support, he staged a coup for his father's throne. Apparently taken off guard by this grossly-disloyal act, David and his officials fled into the wilderness for safety.

OLD ALLIANCES OFTEN DIE HARD, and now that David seemed humiliated and powerless, one person from Saul's clan got a little bold and thought he'd taunt the once-again fugitive. This man's name was Shimei, and he hurled insults, curses, and rocks at David and his men as they fled the city. No doubt, Shimei had been convinced that Absalom's coup had been successful, so there was no way David would ever be returning. Shimei attributed David's suffering to an act of God's judgment and discipline. Over and over, Shimei called him a man of blood. Again, while David did have a reputation for being a fierce military fighter, the Bible does not record a single instance where David took a man's life out of personal revenge. Of course, he had full opportunity to do so with Saul and Nabal—but he left the fate of his oppressors and offenders in the hands of God. Now, here seemed to be yet another opportunity to spill a man's blood over a personal insult during a vulnerable time.

Once again, one of David's loyal followers was more than willing to permanently shut this man up—all the king needed to do was to say the word. But David stayed the hand of his ardent follower because David was confident that God would vindicate him appropriately.

When David got to his destination and was able to refresh himself physically and emotionally, the king drew upon his fugitive experience with Saul that happened decades earlier. He was able to win the hearts of the people of Judah, and he began to create a plan to regain his throne.

When "Sincere Shimei" realized that David was regaining his popularity and position, the former heckler decided it would probably be in his best interests to apologize—or at least to ask the momentum-gathering king to just forget the incident all together.

Abishai, one of David's bodyguards, again volunteered his services. He was the loyal follower who was ready to permanently silence this heckler in the first place—and now he was ready to do it again. In fact, this time, he describes David as "the Lord's anointed," clearly an allusion to David's description of Saul when he was running from the maddening king. Back then, David refused to attack the Lord's anointed—but this hyena mocked David from a distance, hurled insults, and threw stones and dirt at the escaping king. Surely these actions were worthy of death.

But David knew there was nothing to be gained by killing a man who at least admitted that he had sinned. So David promised Shimei, with an oath, that he would never personally put him to death. Once again, David openly blessed one of his enemies.

Now, we know on David's deathbed that he warned Solomon about this unsavory character. The shallowness of Shimei's contrition was never in doubt, and so, as the new king, Solomon should be wary of this man's doublespeak. Solomon gave Shimei a chance to prove his loyalty by staying in Jerusalem. But with the excuse of chasing some escaped slaves, Shimei violated his oath and ran after them. Some scholars think this was nothing but a ruse on Shimei's part. What he really wanted to do was regroup with his former clan and perhaps stir up some dissension against Solomon. But the new king brought a swift end to any possible conspiracy by doing what he said he'd do if Shimei tried to leave the city—Shimei was executed.

OUR WILLINGNESS TO FORGIVE SOMEONE does not need to be based on the prospect that our forgiveness will finally end the matter in God's eyes. Perhaps our involvement with that person will come to an end. Perhaps we will choose to stay in a relationship with that person, for a variety of legitimate reasons. But in these cases, we understand that our level of vulnerability with the person may never be deeper than "maintenance mode."

But just because we have forgiven someone, it doesn't mean that God is finished with that person. That is what Paul means when he implores offended believers—those who have taken all the appropriate steps concerning human justice—to step aside and "leave room for the wrath of God." (Rom. 12:19).

There is still going to be a day of reckoning for that person. Even if that person has repented, the Lord may still correct him—for whomever the Lord loves, he disciplines (Prov. 3:12; Heb. 12:6). And for those who, by their words and actions, show that they want nothing to do with God . . . the day of accountability comes closer with every hour that passes.

To this end, we must now look to the subjects of justice, revenge, and divine retribution.

3The Unexpected Emptiness
of
Human Justice

God has established human systems of justice to deter, restrain, and discipline evildoers. These systems always begin with responsible confrontation and may involve supportive friends and family members, qualified professionals, the police, the military, the secular courts, or church disciplinary councils. We are commanded by God to passionately pursue justice within these established systems of accountability, no matter how ineffective or dissatisfying these time-consuming processes might be.

Ron's story, Part II

"THANK YOU FOR MEETING WITH US, RON. I'm Jonas Carter with the Securities and Exchange Commission, and this is Special Agent Ben Gaiman with the FBI."

"Hello, this is my attorney, Daniel Pena."

"Pleasure to meet you."

Well, thought Ron to himself, *the feeling ain't mutual.*

"A few questions, Ron . . . of course, Mr. Pena, feel free to interrupt at any time. Ron, you claim that you sent several e-mails to your supervisor expressing concern about potential fraudulent claims on your company's books. Is that correct?"

"Yes."

"Did you copy anyone on those e-mails?"

"No."

"Are you aware that when we confiscated your computer, the hard drive was completely reformatted, and all data on that hard drive—including your apparent e-mails—had effectively been destroyed?"

"Yes."

"Are you aware that your supervisor has accused you of destroying that data, and that we have signed affidavits from him stating that you never informed him, either in person, or by e-mail, about the possible fraud that was occurring?"

"Yes, I'm aware of all those things."

"Ron, we hired a firm that specializes in recovering data that has been deleted or destroyed from any hard drive. It's quite an expensive process, but amazingly effective. Did you know that we had taken this step?"

The lawyer's eyes widened. "No, no one told us that you were doing any such thing—what did you find?"

"We discovered the hard drive of a software programmer who apparently played of lot of online chess."

"But that hard drive was definitely in my computer, right?"

"Yes, which of course prompted us to talk to all of your Information Services technicians. We discovered that one of them was told directly by your supervisor to switch the hard drives and then reformat the new one. He was told to destroy yours, but instead, hid it behind a bunch of servers."

"So you have my hard drive?"

"Yes."

"And all of my e-mails?"

"Every single one of them."

"So . . ."

"So, Ron, in light of this new evidence, we are going to dismiss all charges against you in this matter. You were obviously set up, and the SEC does not take kindly to being deceived. I'm no judge, but I imagine if you pursued this matter the company should reimburse your salary for the time you've been suspended, as well as Mr. Pena's fees. I would imagine there would also be some sort of punitive settlement."

A wave of relief washed over Ron, until he remembered what he put in his filing cabinet.

"What about the fish?"

"What fish?"

———————

An innate sense of justice seems to strongly manifest itself during the elementary-school years—when the words "That's not fair!" seem to be repeated *ad nauseum*. Where does this come from?

As human beings, we are created in the image of God—that is to say, we all reflect the attributes of God in a limited and finite way. God is all-knowing, and we have limited knowledge. God is all-powerful, and we have limited power. God exists in His totality at every point in space, and we exist in our totality, in a set, well-defined amount of space (which, for some of us, seems to increase from year to year).

The same could be said about our emotional make-up. During medieval times, several lofty theologians postulated that God was "passionless"— that is, he did not suffer, he did not experience joy— he simply did not experience any emotion whatsoever. Several modern theologians have responded to this type of thinking by using a highly-technical, though still accessible word — *baloney*.

The Scriptures are quite clear that the Spirit of God takes delight and rejoices in His people (Zeph. 3:17) and grieves when people sin (Eph. 4:30). Certainly Jesus felt compassion, annoyance, determination, frustration, excitement, contempt, and of course, gratitude. And, is there any question at all, in anybody's mind, that the Lord gets angry? It seems to me that to suggest God holds back on how He really feels about certain things is difficult to support. So I strongly dismiss the idea that God is emotion-free. In fact, it is because God is a perfectly emotional being that we have any feelings at all—again, because we are created in His image, and therefore reflect who is He is — in limited, finite, and often-abused ways.

One of the primary emotions we reflect from God's image is the overwhelming desire to see justice accomplished. In 2 Thessalonians, the Apostle Paul reminds us that God not only cares about justice, but that judicial equity is a reflection of His very essence. As God is love (1 John 4:8, 16)—that is, his very being reflects the essence of love, God is also just (2 Thess. 2:6)—that is, He will allow no good deed to pass unrewarded, and He will allow no evil deed to pass unpunished, because it is part of His very character to make sure that this happens. The tip of his finger is placed below the exact epicenter of the cosmic scales of justice — and in the end, these scales must and will be perfectly balanced.

Because God is just, and we reflect this part of His essence in our own limited reflection of his emotional essence, we are left with a sense of unsettledness and discomfort whenever we witness or experience injustice. There is something inside of us that says "this needs to be made right — these actions cannot go unanswered — the person who has committed these evil deeds needs to be held accountable."

And God is saying the same thing.

People often push themselves into taking justice into their own hands (that is, taking revenge) because they lack the confidence that justice will be accomplished on their behalf—or pursuing justice is just going to take too long and probably be dissatisfying if it does happen. That's why an ever-increasing confidence in God's justice is absolutely crucial for complete forgiveness to ever take place.

The writer of Hebrews gives us the theological foundation for this idea — "There is no forgiveness without the shedding of blood" (Heb. 9:22). Now obviously here's a verse that can easily be abused. For example . . . on his deathbed, the 19th-century Spanish general Ramón Narvaez was asked if he had forgiven his enemies. "I have no need to forgive my enemies," replied the dying commander, "I have had them all shot."

In contrast, Hebrews 9:22 reminds us of the Old Testament sacrificial system that served as a shadow of Christ's atoning sacrifice. Any sin, even forgiven sin, needs to be countered on the universal scales of justice. When we are absolutely confident that God will make this happen, then we can abandon the idea that somehow we're going to lose our self-respect if we forgive—or that, in some outrageous way, those who have hurt us are somehow going to get away with their damaging behavior.

After motivating and emotionally equipping us to pursue justice, the Lord instructs us, several times throughout the Scriptures, to do that very thing.

"Learn to do right! Seek justice, encourage the oppressed. Defend the cause of the fatherless, plead the case of the widow."
                                                                      —Isaiah 1:17

O house of David, this is what the LORD says: "Administer justice every morning; rescue from the hand of his oppressor the one who has been robbed, or my wrath will break out and burn like fire because of the evil you have done—burn with no one to quench it."
                                                                      —Jeremiah 21:12

"Hate evil, love good; maintain justice in the courts."
                                                                      —Amos 5:15

"He has showed you, O man, what is good. And what does the LORD require of you? To act justly and to love mercy and to walk humbly with your God."
                                                                      —Micah 6:8

"Woe to you Pharisees, because you give God a tenth of your mint, rue and all other kinds of garden herbs, but you neglect justice and the love of God. You should have practiced the latter without leaving the former undone."
                                                                      —Luke 11:42

Human justice, appropriately pursued, serves as a deterrent to evil. While the nightly news seems to be filled with reports of wars and crimes all over the world, these accounts would seem like nothing if God's servant rulers did, in fact, "bear the sword for nothing" (Rom. 13:4). For every assault that is committed, how many do not take place because of the prospect of punishment and retribution by well-armed authorities?

In addition to being a deterrent, human justice can also serve as a vehicle of correction, discipline, and restitution. When all else fails, sometimes only the appropriate punishment, when executed by those who have the authority to do so, is the only thing that can soften the hard-hearted and provoke genuine repentance.

Pleading for justice — permission granted

The Lord told an interesting parable in Luke 18 about a powerless widow who kept bringing her case before an unjust judge, pleading for justice that she could not accomplish on her own.

> *Jesus told his disciples a parable to show them that they should always pray and not give up. He said: "In a certain town there was a judge who neither feared God nor cared about men. And there was a widow in that town who kept coming to him with the plea, 'Grant me justice against my adversary.'*
>
> *"For some time he refused. But finally he said to himself, 'Even though I don't fear God or care about men, yet because this widow keeps bothering me, I will see that she gets justice, so that she won't eventually wear me out with her coming!'"*
>
> *And the Lord said, "Listen to what the unjust judge says. And will not God bring about justice for his chosen ones, who cry out to him day and night? Will he keep putting them off? I tell you, he will see that they get justice, and quickly.*
>
> —Luke 18:1-8a

Let's take a closer look at some of the facts in this story:

1. A widow had been wronged. We don't know the nature of the injustice, but apparently it was grievous enough that she was compelled to seek out justice for herself.

2. The only person with any power to help her was completely calloused and indifferent to her plight. She was dirt poor, so there was no potential for a juicy bribe here. Frankly, he couldn't care less about her or her problem.

3. The judge's apathy did not prevent the widow from consistently and persistently pleading for justice. For the sake of his own sanity, the unjust judge gave in to the widow's demands and accomplished the justice that she sought.
4. The widow was not specific about how she wanted justice to be done; she left that in the hands of the judge. In fact, the sentence he handed down remains a mystery.

This parable is often cited to illustrate the value of persistent prayer (in fact, Luke makes it clear that this is why Jesus told the parable). However, the subject of this prayer parable is often played down. The focus of this "prayer" was not healing or spiritual growth. Someone had been wronged, and this was a petition for justice—pure and simple.

And it is that plea for justice that is foundational to every prayer for retribution in the Scriptures.

THE FAMOUS PHRASE "AN EYE FOR AN EYE, A TOOTH FOR A TOOTH" is repeated three times in the Pentateuch (Exod. 21:24; Lev. 24:20; Deut. 19:21). Many scholars have stated that this standard for justice is meant as a restraint—that no one was to be punished beyond what was appropriate for his crime.

But the phrase also points to a type of "emotional equilibrium" that needs to be restored after an injustice has been committed. Simply put, if a person has deliberately or maliciously created some type of loss in somebody's life, then the offender should suffer a comparable loss.

After all, it only seems right.

In the Sermon on the Mount, however, Jesus responded to this type of thinking in light of His atoning ministry.

> *"You have heard that it was said, 'Eye for eye, and tooth for tooth.' But I tell you, Do not resist an evil person. If someone strikes you on the right cheek, turn to him the other also. And if someone wants to sue you and take your tunic, let him have your cloak as well. If someone forces you to go one mile, go with him two miles. Give to the one who asks you, and do not turn away from the one who wants to borrow from you.*
> —Matthew 5:38-42

Jesus is telling us here that when we are wronged, the first step we are to take is to offer our offenders the opportunity to repent by doing something so shocking, so unexpected, that their conscience is suddenly awakened—if, in fact, it even exists. Our immediate reaction to their insolence is to be one of kindness—and to offer them more than what they initially sought to wrest from us.

However, many Christians have mistakenly interpreted this teaching about turning the other cheek to mean that we are to simply keep ignoring the personal injustices inflicted upon us . . . to just pretend that they didn't happen, or to just keep absorbing the abuse, or to simply accept these slights with martyr-like resignation.

Many scholars have effectively argued that the "turn the other cheek" admonitions of Christ use a tense in the Greek to indicate that these encounters should be isolated events. This insight, coupled with other teachings of Jesus—like the command to plead with justice (as we've seen in Luke 18), his instructions concerning church discipline (in Matt. 18), and statements from the Apostle Paul about giving divisive people no more than two warnings (Titus 3:10)—seem to indicate that turning the other cheek, or giving away your cloak, or going the extra mile, are intended to jumpstart the offender's conscience and to encourage a first shot at repentance. As Solomon and Paul teach, when we do kind things to our enemies, we heap burning coals of fire on their heads—presumably to get them to think about and stop what they're doing (Prov. 25:22; Rom. 12:20).

Again, genuine repentance is a form of justice—or at least a vehicle through which justice can flow. Even the secular courts acknowledge this. Prison sentences are often reduced when the convict expresses some sort of believable remorse—and maximized when there is no compunction. That's one reason why we are commanded to offer our offenders opportunities to repent—and turning the other cheek is to be our first offering to them. If they repent when we stun them in this manner, then there is no need to take the issue any further. Their complete acknowledgment of sin calls upon the death of Christ to balance the scales of justice for their wrongdoing. So justice is fully satisfied.

However, fools and other remorseless-types, who have no conscience, will keep slapping you, keep taking the clothes off your back, and compel you to go mile after mile after extra mile until you drop from exhaustion. And then when you're no longer of any use to them, they'll find someone else to exploit.

So in these instances, turning the other cheek becomes a test that indicates the presence of some sort of conscience in the perpetrator. If no moral sense or remorse appears on the radar screen (again, on the part of the offender), then it's time to set in motion God's systems of accountability, starting with safe, responsible confrontation, and then if necessary, involving the governing authorities or church leadership. We take these next steps in order to keep presenting the offender with opportunities to repent—in ways that may or may not prove meaningful to him.

SIX YEARS AND FIFTY-THREE DAYS after taking the lives of 168 men, women, and children, a young man who hated America was executed for his crime. He had rented a truck, filled it with fertilizer-based explosives, and detonated the makeshift bomb in front of the Murrah Federal Building in Oklahoma City.

Six years and fifty-three days is a long time to wait for justice. The defendant strung out the appeals process for a while, and then abruptly ended his requests. He went out rather quietly, but still remorseless and defiant. He boasted that even after the government took his life, the score would still be 168-to-1.

Many of the victims' fami-

> What if, after turning the other cheek, the slapper does genuinely repent—and then the next week sues you for your cloak—and genuinely repents again—and then the next week compels you to go the extra mile? How long then, do you keep this up?
>
> According to Jesus, 70 x 7 times—in other words, you don't keep track. Hopefully, the person will eventually come around and stop repeating his or her damaging behavior—or it becomes a little less damaging each time. But, as Christians, we are to keep giving them another chance, as long as genuine repentance seems to keep trying to come to the surface.

lies and some of the survivors witnessed this young man's execution, and were asked afterwards if his death gave them any sense of closure. Some felt that it did. They were relieved to know that this particular person was silenced and could no longer hurt them with his arrogant words of defiance and the reduction of their lost children to "collateral damage." However, there were some who bristled at the very concept of closure, knowing that the consequences of this angry man's evil actions would stay with them the rest of their lives. A few of those who watched the lethal injection said, in essence, "That's it? That's all there is? He just falls asleep and I'm left with all of this pain?"

And then, three months later—to the day—after Timothy McVeigh was executed, several angry young men, who also hated America, commandeered four commercial jets and took more than sixteen times the number of lives that the former Gulf War veteran did in his early morning attack.

And we are left wondering, how will justice ever be accomplished in this case? Will we ever be able to apprehend, much less successfully prosecute, every single person who contributed to this tragedy? And, if and when that justice is accomplished, will it bring the closure we so desperately seek? Or—when justice has fully run its course—will we also be saying, "Is that it? Is that all there is?"

So we begin to think . . . maybe we should cross the line of justice, push it just a little further and set aside accountability—just this once. You know, stir up just a little more suffering for these low-lifes. And suddenly we're exploring the dark and foreboding possibility of taking human revenge.

4 The Seduction of Human Revenge

When human justice seems dissatisfying, which it often is, we must not give in to the temptation of taking things into our own hands— namely, pursuing human revenge.

The conclusion to Ron's story . . .

RON'S COMPANY DIDN'T GO BANKRUPT over the fraudulent books, but they certainly had a change in leadership. It would have been a scheduling nightmare to arrange a board meeting in the penitentiary. Even so, Ron decided not to stay with the company, even though they gave him a very generous settlement that involved no litigation whatsoever.

When everything had been settled, Ron decided to go back one last time to see his friends. Of course, when he left the last time, he was told, in no uncertain terms, that he would never be allowed back in the building. Now, someone was holding the door for him. All the people who had averted their eyes the last time he left were now greeting him; some even shook his hand. Finally, he reached his work area, which his co-workers had affectionately called "The Cul-de-Sac" because of the way it was configured. These people were some of his closest friends. None of them averted their eyes when he left—those eyes were all filled with tears. Of course everyone was happy to see Ron again, though they were disappointed that he wasn't coming back.

But no one mentioned anything about a funny smell. When Ron got home after that vengeful stunt, he sunk into an even deeper despair. The only ones who would be hurt by this were these friends. By the time it got really bad, no one he really wanted to disgust would have ever smelled a thing.

One of the last people to say good-bye to him was Mary. She had usually taken it upon herself to keep "The Cul-de-Sac" a little neater than it had to be.

And then it dawned on Ron. Mary had an incredible sense of smell. Ron would often eat chips at his desk, and Mary had a habit of announcing the type and even the brand of the chips he was eating as she walked by the outside of his office—and she was always right.

Ron took her aside and whispered, "Mary, did you get rid of the fish?"

"Yes, as a matter of fact I did—what were you thinking?"

"I was being stupid; I'm sorry."

"About twenty minutes after you left, I caught the first whiff. I couldn't tell at first if they were trout or perch—but I knew they were going to raise a big stink if I didn't get rid of them. Of course, I went right to the filing cabinet and used the master keys to get them out."

"Thank you Mary; you're the best."

"Well, it's okay. And God bless in your new adventure, whatever that turns out to be."

———

WHILE WE ARE STRONGLY COMMANDED BY THE SCRIPTURES to pursue and support justice, we are just as passionately forbidden to take things into our own hands and pursue what is known as revenge.

> "'Do not seek revenge or bear a grudge against one of your people, but love your neighbor as yourself. I am the LORD.'"
>
> —Leviticus 19:18

Consider the Lord's indignation against the Edomites and Philistines for taking for themselves something that only belongs to him—namely, revenge.

> "This is what the Sovereign LORD says: 'Because Edom took revenge on the house of Judah and became very guilty by doing so, therefore this is

*what the Sovereign LORD says: I will stretch out my
hand against Edom and kill its men and their ani-
mals. I will lay it waste, and from Teman to Dedan
they will fall by the sword.* I will take vengeance on
Edom *by the hand of my people Israel, and they will
deal with Edom in accordance with my anger and my
wrath;* they will know my vengeance, *declares the
Sovereign LORD.'"*

"*This is what the Sovereign LORD says:* 'Because
the Philistines acted in vengeance and took
revenge *with malice in their hearts, and with ancient
hostility sought to destroy Judah, therefore this is
what the Sovereign LORD says: I am about to stretch
out my hand against the Philistines, and I will cut off
the Kerethites and destroy those remaining along the
coast. I will carry out great vengeance on them and
punish them in my wrath. Then they will know that
I am the LORD,* when I take vengeance on them.'"
—*Ezekiel 25:12-17 (emphasis added).*

Revenge is the most deceptive of all the forbidden passions. The
typical revenge fantasy always plays itself out perfectly—like many
Hollywood endings encourage us to believe. When implemented, however, the bubble is burst, and the loss we hoped to create in the life of
the offender comes back upon us.

In fact, when most revenge
fantasies are acted out, the
original offender becomes the
victim, and the person who was
hurt becomes the offender. The
reputation you hoped to taint
has now become your own. Or
perhaps this out-of-control
desire pushed you to do some-

> "Having reached the summit
> of his vengeance by the slow
> and tortuous path that he had
> followed, he saw an abyss of
> doubt yawning before him."
> —*The Count of Monte Cristo*
> by Alexandre Dumas

thing illegal, and now you are the one on trial. And now the original
offender, who's soaking in all the sympathy, is relishing this double-
whammy against you that he never expected.

A Monumental Traitor

There was a general in the Revolutionary War that was known for his cunning and military victories. He led the colonists to several early victories against the British, even before George Washington had won any battles. For his heroism, Congress promoted him to brigadier general. Had he continued on this patriotic course, or perhaps even been killed in battle, this general would probably have several monuments to his memory in Washington D.C. and the United States Military Academy (West Point). However, because of one act of revenge, today his name is now synonymous, along with Judas, with being a traitor. That general's name was Benedict Arnold.

General Arnold began to pout because he didn't feel he was getting the recognition he deserved. That, coupled with personal financial pressures, compelled him to sell the plans for the fort at West Point to the British. This would have given the Redcoats the keys to the Hudson River, effectively cutting off the northern colonies from their southern counterparts.

Benedict Arnold gave the plans to a courier, but the British never saw them. The courier was captured and hanged. Benedict Arnold escaped and became an officer for the British and even defeated his former comrades at forts in Virginia and New York. When Cornwallis surrendered at Yorktown, Benedict Arnold escaped again to England, where he lived out the rest of his days in virtual exile, despised by both countries.

What's the difference between justice and revenge?

What then, is the difference between justice and human revenge? The two seem to have similar features—both seek to hold foolish and evil people accountable and to punish them appropriately (in the eyes of the offended). Both seem to offer the prospect of deterrence, correction, discipline, and restitution.

But the pursuit of one is clearly commanded by Scripture, and one is clearly forbidden. Why is that? Perhaps we can answer this question by offering an analogy.

Human revenge is to justice as adultery is to marriage.

Some believe that if a husband or wife cannot find certain emotional needs being met in the marriage relationship, then that person is justified in attempting to gratify those needs extra-maritally. If one is not experiencing the affection he or she expected from a spouse, then perhaps that intimacy can be found in the arms of another.

The mental gymnastics that take place when one toys with an affair are similar to the thought processes of the person who considers crossing the clear line between justice and revenge.

As we stated earlier, sometimes justice does not provide the closure we so desperately seek. Yeah, sure, the offender is going to be embarrassed, or fined, or will spend some time in jail—but is that enough? And if it's not going to be enough, shouldn't we pursue more?

In addition, justice, appropriately pursued, may take years. A seriously wounded person might ask, *What am I supposed to do with this aching need for vindication while I wait for this person to bear the full brunt of his actions—and who may very well get off because of a technicality? What if he pleads temporary insanity and the jury buys it? What if the person who has hurt me hasn't done anything illegal and so there never will be any opportunity to "get my day in court"? What then?*

Well, the victim begins to think, *maybe if I take this into my own hands, we can accelerate the process a bit, and be assured that this bottom-dweller is going to get exactly what he deserves. No need to sustain the burden of proof—I have all the proof I need. His evil and malicious motives are as plain as the pimples on his nose. I cannot wait for a process that may, in the end, fail me. Yes, I will take justice* (which has now become revenge) *into my own hands.*

This type of thinking can take place over months, or within a split second. The human mind is remarkable in its ability to quickly manipulate information and form an opinion — no claims to remarkable accuracy, of course, but the speed and complexity of such thinking is quite amazing.

Let's take a look at one last scenario in David's life to see how this "man after God's own heart" dealt with the temptation of revenge during a time of heightened vulnerability.

Out of the frying pan and into the fire

Soon after David had his close encounter with Nabal, Saul was again hot on David's trail. In fact, David's near-slaughter of Nabal and his servants is preceded and followed by near-death encounters with Saul—near-death for the older king, that is. Twice, David is given the opportunity to take justice into his own hands and kill the man who would surely kill him if he had the chance—and David did not do it. Even the men around David insisted that these opportunities must be of the Lord, and he'd be foolish to let them go. But amazingly, he trusts the Lord for vindication, and allows Saul to go free—leaving the door open, of course, to be pursued by the insane monarch once the king has another change of mind.

In the first encounter, before the incident with Nabal, David had gotten a short reprieve from Saul's pursuit because the old king was distracted by a Philistine raid back home. At the time, they were only on opposite sides of the same hill. Just as Saul and his men were about to close in, the king received a report that the Philistines were raiding the land. So he broke off his pursuit to take care of the problem. This gave David and his men a few days to regroup—but they could hardly relax.

After the Philistine problem was brought under control, Saul received a report about David's whereabouts, and immediately took his 3000 men to hunt the young man down. This time, the two got even closer than the last encounter, but David was the only one who knew it. David and his men were hiding in a cave when Saul entered to "relieve himself"—quite possibly, Saul also lay down to rest, and probably fell asleep.

Instead of cutting his throat, as David's men urged him to do, all he did was cut a small swatch of cloth from Saul's robe to prove how close he came. David was so sensitive about not taking any sort of vengeful action against the Lord's anointed, he was even conscience-stricken about this little "receipt" of his non-fatal action.

When Saul was at a safe distance, David called out to him and challenged the king's errant beliefs about David's intentions. The fact that David had this swatch proved he could have killed the king, but did not. He had no interest in harming the king or in taking the throne by force.

Then David said a profound thing to Saul in this exchange that reflects the foundational truth of this book—"May the Lord judge between you and me." David had long since given up on having any sort of healthy relationship with this madman. He had done everything humanly possible to be reconciled with him but realized this was going to be impossible. There was no court of justice between the king and this now-common servant, so David had reached the point where he said, "I have done all that I possibly can, and this relationship cannot be healed."

Clearly, Saul had no interest in reconciliation either, but he was determined to eliminate this perceived threat to his position—with or without the Lord's blessing. At one point, Saul even said to those around him, "God has handed [David] over to me . . ." (1 Sam. 23:7), when in fact the Lord had done no such thing. But that's how the remorseless mind thinks — it interprets every event, consequence and circumstance in its favor. Humanly speaking, there's no changing its mind . . . at least not permanently.

David's pronouncement of calling on the Lord to judge between two opposing parties was a common one in Scripture. It effectively announced the end of all human negotiation, and now the result was to be left in the hands of God. Laban made this same pronouncement as he sealed an agreement with his son-in-law, Jacob (Gen. 31:53). Jepthah attempted to avert battle with the Ammonites by invoking this pronouncement (Judg. 11:27). Solomon asked the Lord to judge between his servants in his prayer to dedicate the temple (1 Kings 8:32). Isaiah and Micah declared that the Lord would one day settle disputes between nations (Isa. 2:4; Mic. 4:3). And this little phrase was even used to end a fight between arguing spouses (Gen. 16:5).

SEVERAL YEARS AGO I WAS INVOLVED IN A CHURCH that was going through a bit of a leadership crisis. The issues at hand involved the roles and qualifications of elders in the church. I had respectfully expressed my concerns to the existing church leadership, and they responded to my concerns in an exemplary way by assigning one of the elders to engage me in an extended dialogue on the subject.

We got together over coffee once in awhile, and since we both liked to write, we often exchanged letters. Since this was an issue over which reasonable Christians have disagreed, we simply found ourselves articulating the views of our respective camps.

After a few weeks, I tried to wrap up the discussion by saying, "Sam, I think we've said all we can to each other—though the discussion has been lively and engaging, I haven't convinced you and you haven't convinced me — we'll just have to wait for the Lord to judge between us."

I was surprised at how strongly he responded to that last statement.

"Hey, there's no need to go that far, for heaven's sake. We can work this out—we don't have to have God intervene." It was as if I had gone too far and pulled rank on him! I didn't dig in my heels and insist that I was right . . . or that the Lord was definitely going to back me up on this one. Perhaps God would expose my own incorrect assumptions and conclusions. We simply had an honest disagreement. We did everything we could to work it out—and now had to leave it in the Lord's hands. But my friend would have none of that, at least initially, because he admitted that he didn't want to grapple with the prospect that one day every belief, attitude, motivation, argument, and philosophical position that he held, and I held, would be ruthlessly judged and compared to God's perfect standard.

David made this pronouncement ("May the Lord judge between us") twice in this confrontational exchange with Saul. And then David makes it clear what he considers to be his responsibility and God's responsibility.

> May the LORD avenge the wrongs you have done
> to me, but my hand will not touch you.
> —1 Samuel 24:12

This captures the real-world essence and character of the man who wrote "The Psalms of Rage." First, David does not downplay the fact that he is clearly being wronged—and he's telling it straight to the offender's face. What he does *not* say is that, because he has been wronged, he is now entitled to take revenge.

On two occasions, David clearly had an opportunity to take justice into his own hands—even though there was no system of justice in place at the time for exposing the wrongdoing of a powerful ruler. The only ones who seem to get away with confronting a king (and even then, not always) were the prophets—and Samuel was dead. Instead, David expresses confidence in God's willingness to exact revenge on his behalf. Not just punish, discipline, or rebuke—he asks God to avenge him. David calls upon God to consider his complaint, and finding him justified, to vindicate him.

On the second similar pursuit (after "Honest Saul" had promised to leave him alone), David expressed some of his thoughts to Abishai, one of his bodyguards, about what God might allow to happen to the older king.

> *The LORD himself will strike him; either his time*
> *will come and he will die, or he will go into battle*
> *and perish. But the LORD forbid that I should lay a*
> *hand on the LORD's anointed.*
> *—1 Samuel 26:10-11*

David is considerably more impassioned and explicit about what might happen to those who have hurt him in his prayers for retribution, but the sentiment is the same: *Vengeance belongs to the Lord, so God forbid that I should raise my hand in an act of personal revenge.*

It is also interesting to note David's reluctance to believe Saul's apparently-penitent pleas—at least not without any positive actions to back them up.

> *Then Saul said, "I have sinned. Come back,*
> *David my son. Because you considered my life pre-*
> *cious today, I will not try to harm you again. Surely*
> *I have acted like a fool and have erred greatly."*
>
> *"Here is the king's spear," David answered. "Let*
> *one of your young men come over and get it."*
> *—1 Samuel 26:21-22*

First, Saul admits that he has sinned and acted foolishly—but then invites David to come home. To which David essentially replies, "Forget about it . . . if you want your spear back, have someone come over here and retrieve it. But I'm not coming anywhere near you."

Saul was apparently so moved by David's mercy in the first encounter, that he cried out loud. But, even though he said he was sorry, he still didn't want his legacy to suffer, so he asked David to promise that Saul's name would be remembered. And David graciously accepted his request and openly blessed his enemy—even while he kept a safe distance.

After successfully evading Saul for a second time, David understandably hit a wall of despair. As when Elijah was pursued by Ahab and Jezebel, David had doubts about how long he could keep being chased. So he decided to send himself into exile, into the land of Saul's enemies, the Philistines, where the cowardly king would never go.

Shortly after Saul returned, he visited the witch of Endor where he got the first hint that the end was near. As David predicted, Saul was killed in the context of a battle (in fact, he took his own life), and his pursuit of David was finally over.

David's time of vindication was near . . . but there would be other enemies, other pursuits, other times of despair, and other compelling periods of looking to God for retribution and vindication. And to increase his confidence during these trying times, David offered up what we have called, "The Psalms of Rage."

WHAT BELONGS TO GOD, AND TO GOD ALONE, cannot be wrong, immoral, or anything less than perfect.

[Divine] revenge fits this category.

> "It is mine to avenge; I will repay. In due time their foot will slip; their day of disaster is near and their doom rushes upon them."
> —Deuteronomy 32:35

> Do not take revenge, my friends, but leave room for God's wrath, for it is written: "It is mine to avenge; I will repay," says the Lord.
> —Romans 12:19

Revenge, like jealousy, is an emotion that is so highly-charged, so capable of doing incredible damage, that only God can handle it. In the mind of a human being, the desire for revenge—if allowed to ferment—can grow into something that expands far beyond his or her capacity to contain.

Within the sovereign plan of God, however, divine retribution is never anything less than true and just . . . and eternally effective.

We now turn our attention and confidence to this immutable truth.

5The Promise of Divine Retribution

God promises to balance the scales of justice for every evil act, from the careless word to the destruction of human life. Our ability to forgive the unrepentant is directly tied to our emotional confidence in God's willingness to do this very thing: to pursue and accomplish justice on our behalf.

Bill's Painting

One of my favorite paintings was done by a friend of mine named Bill. He came by my office one day to show me the painting and to ask my opinion about the Scripture text he was going to use. When I first saw the piece, I immediately knew that this was something I wanted on my office wall—so that I could be reminded of its message every single day.

The name of the painting is *Who Do You Say That I Am?* In the foreground is a picture of Christ with his scarred back to the viewer. In the background are the faces of several famous people in history . . . some living, some dead. The faces included those of Socrates, Alexander the Great, Genghis Khan, George Washington, Nero, King Henry VIII, Darwin, Napoleon, Mao Tse-tung, Hitler, Stalin, Mahatma Gandhi, Abraham Lincoln, Idi Amin, Lenin, the Dalai Lama, Madeline Murray O'Hare, Fidel Castro, Menachem Begin, Yasser Arafat, Mother Theresa, Saddam Hussein, Princess Diana . . . and others.

The message of the painting is that every one of those people will one day answer to Christ. The worldviews that they held and taught will be compared to Jesus' teachings—and judged accordingly.

And, of course, because of Bill's talent, I am compelled to picture myself in that painting—because one day I will be held to the same standard.

About a year after Bill came to show me the painting, I walked into the office to find about 30 people standing in a circle. Some were holding hands. Many of them were crying, and that's always a bad sign. Someone was praying, but I couldn't quite make out what happened. As quietly as I could, I asked a co-worker what happened. My friend Bill, at the age of 42, had had a massive heart attack and died.

The next day we found out what happened. Bill had been giving a television interview because he had been asked to promote his paintings. They had been getting a lot of critical acclaim. In fact, a Russian official bought one of Bill's paintings and hung it in his office in the Kremlin. The interview seemed to go fine, but as soon as they were done, Bill said, "I'm not feeling well" — and then he collapsed. They couldn't revive him. We all knew that Bill had struggled with a congenital heart condition all his life. We all thought the doctors had things under control.

So much for human control.

That television interview was shown at Bill's memorial service. Watching that video was one of the most sobering experiences of my life. Here I am, watching a man speak his last words, having no idea that within the next ten minutes, he was going to be in the presence of God. And, because Bill was a man of deep and abiding faith, he spent those last words acknowledging that God was the source of every creative thought he ever had. Thousands of people obviously enjoyed Bill's gifts and abilities, but he never forgot where they came from, or who sustained them.

So Bill joined the people in that picture—as you and I will do one day. There will be a day of reckoning for everyone—believer and unbeliever—where we will all have to give an account.

Each and every person—no exceptions.

Beyond all you could imagine or even think . . .

As we've said before, our ability to forgive the unrepentant (that is, to emotionally transfer the painful debts that they have created in our lives to the Lord's repayment plan), is inextricably tied to our confidence in God's willingness to accomplish justice on our behalf. If that confidence wanes, we may begin to consider ways to make that person "suffer as I have suffered." However, there's no punishment that you can imagine happening to the remorseless people in your life that God hasn't already implemented in other contexts . . . or will eventually.

To paraphrase Jesus in Matthew 18:6, "If you cause a vulnerable person to stumble [namely, a child], it will be *better* for someone to put you in a boat, head out for the deepest part of ocean, tie a fifty-pound cement doughnut around your neck, and toss you overboard."

He didn't say that's what would happen to the person who hurt a kid — He said that would be *preferred over* what was really going to happen to such a culprit.

Along these lines, Deuteronomy 28 predicted what would happen to the people of Israel if they continued down the path of unacknowledged sin. And every single thing described in this passage eventually did happen to them.

Fast forward to the book of Revelation. Revelation 16 describes the seven bowls of God's wrath—a fiery cocktail of scorching heat, blood, boils, darkness, earthquakes, and 100-pound hailstones (imagine cement bags falling from the sky). The excruciating pain of the defiant targets that this passage describes is quite graphic. But the recipients' continued refusal to repent is even more amazing. Here they are, bearing the full consequential brunt of their sin—and all they're doing is digging their heels in deeper.

The central truth of these two passages (and the hundreds of similar verses in the Bible) describing God's earthly discipline is summed up in Revelation 16:7 — "Yes, Lord God Almighty, true and just are your judgments. " These are not the actions of some malevolent mythological figure who feels slighted. There's nothing false about them—not a single punitive action is based on some trumped-up charge. In the case of God's judgment—by one who knows the hidden motives of each person's heart—there isn't the slightest room here for reasonable doubt. There's nothing unjust about these judgments—they will balance the cosmic scales of justice perfectly.

All of these earthly judgments, of course, are but a shadow of what will happen on the Final Day of Judgment. This Day of the Lord is a prominent theme that is woven throughout the Scriptures (see Isa. 13:6, 9; Ezek. 13:5; 30:3; Joel 1:15; 2:1, 11, 31; 3:14; Amos 5:18-20; Obad. 15; Zeph. 1:7, 14; Zech. 14:1; Mal. 4:5; Acts 2:20; 1 Cor. 5:5; 2 Cor. 1:14; 1 Thess. 5:2; 2 Thess. 2:2; 2 Pet. 3:10.) Jesus referred to it frequently throughout his earthly ministry, and of course, its final description is articulated, appropriately enough, in the Book of Revelation (namely, chapter 20).

Choosing Hell over Heaven

Like many Christians, I struggled for years with the concept of hell even existing . . . much less it being a place where souls are thrown into fiery caverns where they burn, much like Moses' bush in the wilderness, without being consumed. Many modern theologians have attempted to soften the concept of eternal torment by reducing hell to the act of divine annihilation. According to this view, God waves his hand and the wicked simply stop existing. [To the secular existentialist, it must be said, there is no more terrifying fate than to have your existence wiped out.] But it seems to me that the annihilationists have not adequately dealt with verses such as Revelation 14:11, "And the smoke of their torment rises for ever and ever," and Jesus' description of hell, a place "where 'their worm does not die, and the fire is not quenched'" (Mark 9:48). Hell is a forever place and the remorseless who end up there stay there for eternity.

Granted, there is no passing of "time" in eternity, so the state of the wicked, and the glorified, for that matter, is simply an ongoing sense of the Present—where there is no past or future, only "now." So in the minds of the eternally tormented, there will be no thought of "How long have I been here, and how long will this go on?" but rather, "This is my state, and there is no other."

Jesus also says that it will be more tolerable for some (of the wicked) than others on the Day of Judgment (Matt. 10:15; Matt. 11:22-24). So, as poetically reflected in Dante's *Divine Comedy*, other Scriptures support the idea that there are degrees of punishment in hell as there are degrees of reward in heaven (see Ezek. 16:48-61, Luke 12:47-48, and Rev. 20:12-13). Even so, how can we swallow the concept of such a final and ongoing end — even for the worst of sinners?

Though I have not fully grasped the concept, I believe the answer lies somewhere in the premise of C. S. Lewis' novel, *The Great Divorce*. In this fictional account of the afterlife, a busload of hell-entrenched sinners are given the opportunity to enter into heaven, but want nothing to do with the place—or more specifically, with the guy who runs the place. Lewis postulates that God will say to the remorseless, "Thy will be done." Again, in ways that I still do not fully understand, the remorseless choose hell over heaven, because they have finally seen God in all of His sovereign glory . . . and want nothing to do with him. They reflect the attitude that Milton attributes to Satan in *Paradise Lost*—"better to reign in hell than to serve in heaven." So God, in essence, created a place where He was not (and that is hardly even conceivable), where there is no one reigning, but simply billions of isolated souls, journeying deeper and deeper into their self-justification, only to become more and more alone.

> The Present is the point at which Time touches Eternity. Of the present moment — and of it only—humans have an experience analogous to the experience which God has of reality as a whole; in it alone, freedom and actuality are offered them. He would therefore have them continually concerned either with Eternity (which means being concerned with Him) or with the Present—either meditating on their eternal union with, or separation from, Himself—or else obeying the present voice of conscience, bearing the present cross, receiving the present grace, giving thanks for the present pleasure.
>
> C. S. Lewis

But what if the person who continues to hurt you is also a believer. What then? Does he simply pull out his "Get-Out-of-Hell-Free" card (at no cost to him, anyway)—and enter into the pearly gates without ever answering for his crime?

No, that would make a mockery of grace, and Jude warns us to beware of those who use the grace of God as a license to sin. Even for believers, there is a time of divine evaluation.

Protestant Purgatory

Some of my Catholic friends believe that after death, many Christian souls go to a place called purgatory—it's not hell, but it's still a terrifying place (at least in Catholic doctrine).

Purgatory is the topic of Dante's "Purgatorio" — Part 2 of his *Divine Comedy*—the first and most popular being "Inferno," which provides an elaborate description of the levels of hell and its increasingly painful levels of torment. Part 3, "Paradiso," presents the medieval poet's vision of heaven.

In purgatory, according to Roman Catholic belief, the soul undergoes a period of cleansing, and—one might say—atonement—for the sins he committed in his lifetime. The suffering can be intense, but it's not a place of abandonment and hopelessness. Again, it is portrayed as a place of cleansing and preparation for the believing soul's entrance into heaven.

In medieval times, the frightful concept of purgatory was often abused by the religious leaders. Some of them convinced the masses that it was possible to "cut the time" that a relative or friend's soul had to spend in purgatory by making a small contribution to the church. A Dominican monk named Johann Tetzel made up a little jingle to advertise the indulgences: "As soon as the coin in the coffer rings, a soul from purgatory springs." Soon the contribution scam evolved from springing others from purgatory to cutting off a few years from your own cleansing sentence. The Reformers effectively squashed any such concept of any works-based pre-heaven cleansing, and there was new and refreshing emphasis on the grace of God.

Protestants have typically rejected the existence of purgatory because the process implies that the soul can do something to atone for its own sins. Of course, the hew and cry of the Reformers, such as Luther and Calvin, made it clear that only the blood of Christ atones for sin—and the soul that has been saved, by the grace of God, gains entrance into heaven immediately after the moment of physical death.

To be absent from the body is to be present with
the Lord. (see 2 Corinthians 5:8)

Like all good things, however, even grace can be abused. Jude warns believers today to be on the lookout "for godless men, who change the grace of our God into a license for immorality" (Jude 4). Some people think, quite incorrectly, that once people are saved, they have the freedom to do whatever they wish without any eternal consequences. If people confront them, they just pull out the "grace card"—a quick, nondescript confession—and boom—the slate is wiped clean (in their mind). As far as they're concerned, they'll never have to face any sort of consequences for their insensitive acts.

Even some people who don't abuse grace think there isn't going to be any sort of judgment of Christians. Didn't Paul say "Therefore, there is now no condemnation for those who are in Christ Jesus," (Rom. 8:1) . . . and "If we judged ourselves, we would not come under judgment" (1 Cor. 11:31). In times of grief, we hear this understandable sentiment in the conversations of the friends and family who have just lost a believing loved one. "He's in heaven now—all his tears have been wiped away." No mention of examination—nothing but paradise. Of course, in times of mourning, such talk is inappropriate. And, frankly, the "test results" of another believer's life are none of our business.

But the Scriptures are clear. There is a time of judgment for Christians, and it is a fiery process. Granted, the person's salvation is not at stake, and there's nothing atoning about the event. But it clearly is a time of evaluation and judgment, and Paul describes it in 1 Corinthians 3.

> By the grace God has given me, I laid a foundation as an expert builder, and someone else is building on it. But each one should be careful how he builds. For no one can lay any foundation other than the one already laid, which is Jesus Christ. If any man builds on this foundation using gold, silver, costly stones, wood, hay or straw, his work will be shown for what it is, because the Day will bring it to light. It will be revealed with fire, and the fire will test the quality of each man's work. If what he has built survives, he will receive his reward. If it is burned up, he will suffer loss; he himself will be saved, but only as one escaping through the flames.
> —1 Corinthians 3:10-15

In theological circles, this is often called The Bema Seat judgment, named after a raised platform in first-century market squares where quick judgments were often rendered. Pilate probably sat in such a place when he interrogated Jesus (Matt. 27:19; John 19:13). And Paul reminded the believers in Rome (and us) that "we will all stand before God's judgment seat" (Rom. 14:10). Some scholars have separated the judgment of the wicked from the judgment of believers—but it seems that if, on the final Day of Judgment, the goats are separated from the sheep, then the full spectrum of belief to unbelief is represented during that terrifying and glorious event.

According to Paul in 1 Corinthians 3, the believer's "life" as it were, is placed in a figurative furnace to test the quality of the "materials" he or she used while building a life on the foundation of repentance and belief in Jesus Christ. Apparently there is a wide variety of materials to chose from—from precious metals and jewels to brittle, strawlike stubble.

Paul's bent is clearly one of quality here; the nature of the materials is what's being tested. Obviously, gold, silver, and precious stones will hold up to any level of heat—and when they pass through, they represent different levels of value. Wood, hay, or straw—on the other hand, are going to leave nothing behind but ashes.

I don't think these materials necessarily represent an amount or even certain types of good deeds—but rather the *attitude* in which they were done. Paul often attaches attitudes to particular duties of Christians—not just to give or show mercy—but to do so "cheerfully" (Rom. 12:8; 2 Cor. 9:7)—not just to lead, but to do so "diligently" (Rom. 12:8)—and, of course, 1 Corinthians 13 is all about the relationship of our actions to the genuineness of the love behind them.

All this is to say that nobody gets away with anything—even believers. So the God who promises justice is also ready to call to account those obnoxious, indifferent, insensitive—but nonetheless saved—people in our lives.

Not all get earthly justice

Jesus once acknowledged to a hostile crowd that during the time of Elijah and Elisha, there were many widows and lepers who did not receive supernatural help—there were only two. The impoverished Zarephathian widow and Naaman the leper were healed by God through the prophets—but many others suffered the ill effects of famine and the nerve-destroying disease.

Along these lines, I think we can safely say that there are many who will not receive the full earthly justice that they deserve. In the best of all possible worlds—namely one in which men are given the freedom and responsibility to obey or reject God—powerful, evil people obviously do exist. The poor who are innocent often cannot hire lawyers to aggressively fight for them. And the elite who are clearly guilty can, and often do, hire the lawyers (whom the poor cannot afford) to keep them out of trouble. The really shrewd offenders know how to keep any responsibility from being traced back to them at all.

Asaph, one of the psalmists, was one of the people who had little hope of experiencing the earthly justice that was due to him—or perhaps to the people that he loved. He began to wonder why he expended so much effort to keep his nose clean when he was surrounded by corrupt individuals who did not seem to have a care in the world—and never seemed to suffer any consequences for their wrongdoing.

Psalm 73–A Psalm of Asaph

Surely God is good to Israel, to those who are pure in heart.

But as for me, my feet had almost slipped; I had nearly lost my foothold.

For I envied the arrogant when I saw the prosperity of the wicked.

They have no struggles; their bodies are healthy and strong.

They are free from the burdens common to man; they are not plagued by human ills.

Therefore pride is their necklace; they clothe themselves with violence.

From their callous hearts comes iniquity; the evil conceits of their minds know no limits.

They scoff, and speak with malice; in their arrogance they threaten oppression.

Their mouths lay claim to heaven, and their tongues take possession of the earth.

Therefore their people turn to them and drink up waters in abundance.

They say, "How can God know? Does the Most High have knowledge?"

This is what the wicked are like—always care-free, they increase in wealth.

Surely in vain have I kept my heart pure; in vain have I washed my hands in innocence.

All day long I have been plagued; I have been punished every morning.

If I had said, "I will speak thus," I would have betrayed your children.

When I tried to understand all this, it was oppressive to me till I entered the sanctuary of God; then I understood their final destiny.

When Asaph finally was able to see the final end of these arrogant people—when an ever-increasing confidence in God's ultimate justice started to come upon him—he found that he was better able to cope with the defiance and indifference of those who cared nothing about the pain they were creating in other people's lives.

Surely you place them on slippery ground; you cast them down to ruin.

How suddenly are they destroyed, completely swept away by terrors!

As a dream when one awakes, so when you arise, O Lord, you will despise them as fantasies.

When my heart was grieved and my spirit embittered,

I was senseless and ignorant; I was a brute beast before you.

Yet I am always with you; you hold me by my right hand.

*You guide me with your counsel, and afterward
you will take me into glory.*

*Whom have I in heaven but you? And earth has
nothing I desire besides you.*

*My flesh and my heart may fail, but God is the
strength of my heart and my portion forever.*

*Those who are far from you will perish; you
destroy all who are unfaithful to you.*

*But as for me, it is good to be near God. I have
made the Sovereign LORD my refuge; I will tell of all
your deeds.*

Asaph understood that the types of calamities promised in
Deuteronomy 28 would eventually come upon these people. If it happened in this life or the next, would it really matter? For some fools
and other evil folks, they do taste the consequences of their actions
in this life. They have alienated the people (spouses, children,
friends, co-workers) who once cared about them—but eventually,
they find themselves alone—deeply embittered, and claiming that no
one really understands them. When many of them eventually stand
before God, their defiance will continue, and they will blame others,
and even the Lord, for their wasted lives.

When we begin to understand the eventual terrifying end of the
remorseless, whether it comes in this life or the next, we may find that
our feelings of envy and resentment begin to dissipate. When these
feelings eventually go away, those who have been hurt by the wicked
may experience a type of numbing indifference about what happens to
them.

For some, as the picture of the eventual end of the wicked grows even
clearer, they might find themselves feeling sorry for these offenders—
but still thinking, "Hey, they've had ample opportunity to turn around,
so, there's nothing more I can do."

Occasionally, these feelings move from feeling sorry for these folks,
to actually asking God to be merciful to them—and not to hold certain
sins against them. Certainly this was true of Jesus on the cross, who
asked His father to forgive those who had no idea that they were extin-
guishing the life of God's Son. It seems that the centurion was the only
one of Jesus' executioners who eventually understood what he had

contributed to. Of course, Jesus was able to request forgiveness for his impenitent, but ignorant tormentors because of his unwavering confidence in God as His Supreme Justice.

> *To this you were called, because Christ suffered for you, leaving you an example, that you should follow in his steps . . . When they hurled their insults at him, he did not retaliate; when he suffered, he made no threats.* Instead, he entrusted himself to him who judges justly.
> —1 Peter 2:21, 23

We also see this type of pleading from Stephen, the first Christian martyr, who asked God not to hold the sin of his murder against his executioners—namely, I think, because Stephen was given a glimpse of Jesus standing at his judgment seat, and knew that a horrible and terrifying fate awaited those who had rejected the redeeming words of Moses and the prophets.

DOWN TO THE LAST DAY, even the last hour now. I'm an old man, lonely and unloved, sick and hurting and tired of living. I am ready for the hereafter; it has to be better than this . . . My assets exceed eleven billion dollars. I own silver in Nevada and copper in Montana and coffee in Kenya and coal in Angola and rubber in Malaysia and natural gas in Texas and crude oil in Indonesia and steel in China . . . I had three families—three ex-wives who bore seven children, six of whom are still alive and doing all they can to torment me. To the best of my knowledge, I fathered all seven, and buried one. I should say his mother buried him. I was out of the country . . . I am estranged from all the wives and all the children. They're gathering here today because I'm dying and it's time to divide the money.

Troy Phelan

in John Grisham's novel, *The Testament*

The Promise of Vindication

In ancient times, when a king was victorious in battle against an exceptionally vicious and oppressive enemy, he would often parade his defeated foes, especially the rival king, in front of the cheering crowds.

The procession would often end at a lavish banquet where the conquered enemies would be tied to pillars to watch their conquerors celebrate.

David was probably alluding to this practice when he wrote in Psalm 23, "Thou preparest a table before me in the presence of mine enemies." In essence, David is saying the Lord would vindicate him in front of those who had caused him great suffering. This sentiment is reflected in the Lord's promise to the Christians at the church of Philadelphia when He says in regard to their remorseless enemies—"I will make them come and fall down at your feet and acknowledge that I have loved you" (Rev. 3:9). This promise of acknowledgment and vindication is seen throughout the Scriptures, and the psalmists frequently call upon the Lord to act upon this promise on their behalf.

THE INEVITABLE PROSPECT OF GOD'S PERFECT JUSTICE is what enables the victims of remorseless offenders to abandon all thoughts of forbidden revenge. In fact, it is upon the basis of that divine justice that forgiveness even becomes a possibility. Our ability to forgive grows as our confidence in God's perfect justice increases.

Now we are ready to take a look at the cries for retribution or "imprecatory" prayers of David and others in the Bible as they seek to gain an unwavering confidence in God's perfect justice.

6 The Psalms of Rage
and God's Response to
Other Prayers for Retribution

The prayers of retribution, offered by David and other believers in the Old and New Testament, are God-endorsed attempts to gain a renewed sense of confidence in the Lord's perfect justice.

Compare these prayers . . .

Which of these prayers would you consider to be more "godly"?

Which of these prayers would you be more likely to offer?

Prayer #1

O Lord, remember not only the men and women of good will, but also those of ill will. But do not remember all the suffering they inflicted on us; remember the fruits we have bought, thanks to this suffering—our comradeship, our loyalty, our courage, our generosity, the greatness of heart which as grown out of all this, and when they come to judgment let all the fruits which we have borne be their forgiveness.

Prayer written by an unknown prisoner of Ravensbruck concentration camp, and left by the body of a dead child.

or,

Prayer #2

Destroy thou them, O God.

Let their way be dark and slippery. May ruin overtake them by surprise . . . may they fall into the pit, to their ruin.

In your faithfulness destroy them. Let death seize upon them, and let them go down quick into hell.

Consume them in wrath, consume them, that they may not be. Pour out thine indignation upon them, and let thy wrathful anger take hold of them.

Add iniquity unto their iniquity: and let them not come into thy righteousness.

Let them be blotted out of the book of the living, and not be written with the righteous. Pour out thy wrath upon the heathen that have not known thee.

Let the sinners be consumed out of the earth, and let the wicked be no more.

Excerpts from "The Psalms of Rage" (KJV)

Of course, the question of whether or not these prayers are "godly" is a tricky one . . . Prayer #1 reflects a level of graciousness and mercy one might expect from the most spiritually-mature among us. The second prayer is straight from the Scriptures—these excerpts are taken from the prayerful petitions of King David. These are what are known as the "imprecatory" prayers, or as we will call them, "The Psalms of Rage." Some of these psalms are even found in *The Book of Common Prayer.* They capture the essence of David's response to evil—specifically the type of evil that calls itself good.

The following Psalms have some sort of imprecatory feature or appeal for vindication in them:

> *5, 6, 7, 10, 11, 17, 23, 25, 28, 31, 35, 40, 41,*
> *54, 55, 56, 58, 59, 63, 68, 70, 71, 73, 74, 79,*
> *83, 94, 97, 104, 109, 119, 120, 129, 137, 139,*
> *140, 141, 143, 149*

That's 39 out of 150, or 26%—more than one fourth of the Psalter.

In order to better understand these psalms, we've taken a look at the life of their primary author, namely King David, the second monarch of Israel. We've been able to look at the types of events in David's life that might have provoked these virulent words—and compared these ardent prayers with how he dealt with these enemies in real life.

DAVID IS ONE OF THE MORE fascinating characters in the Bible because we have so much personal information about him. Not only do we have a record of his many adventures, but we're also given insight into what was happening in his head and heart *while* they were happening.

In all of David's roles—shepherd, fugitive, conqueror, husband, father, and king—we don't often see him in the role of teacher. Certainly, Solomon had a reputation as a great teacher, but I think this son of David got his passion for instruction from his father.

David knew that the eyes of the nation were on him. He saw that the history of Israel, warts and all, had been preserved in sacred books such as the Pentateuch. It's even possible that the book of Judges was being composed or had even been finished by the time David had ascended to power—and that book certainly had very little to hide.

Ancient kings often composed chronicles about their battles, victories, and exploits. But these stories often highlighted only the virtues and successes of these rulers. Any scribe who even attempted to expose the less-desirable characteristics of the emperor, much less his failures as a leader, usually wasn't allowed to stick around for very long. So you're not going to find any sort of heart-rending prose inscribed on the side of a pyramid as some Pharaoh pours out his soul about the pressure of holding up and defending an empire. Throughout ancient history, and even in the chronicles of Israel's and Judah's kings, we see absolute power blinding these rulers to their own faults and weaknesses—and this lack of introspective vision proved to be the downfall of each and every one of them.

Not so with David. While he stumbled many times during his career, he was consistently able to re-center himself (by the grace of God), and get back on track with his Heavenly Father. David's psalms, especially the imprecatory prayers, reflect the full spectrum of human emotion in his roller coaster life—from wonder to bewilderment, remorse to inner peace, longing to satisfaction. In these psalms, we are privileged to see the heart of a very powerful man, a man after God's own heart, whose ultimate focus in life is glorifying God.

However, since there is no recorded response from God to the imprecatory psalms of David, many Christians are prone to dismiss them as pre-grace, carnal, vindictive, or mere exaggeration.

The imprecatory prayers of other Old and New Testament saints

But David was not the only one in the Bible to offer such prayers. The Scriptures also include similar petitions by other Old and New Testament saints for which there is a clear response from God. For example, consider the supplications offered by Jeremiah, Habakkuk, and the saints of Revelation 6. If the intent of these prayers was ungodly, we would expect the Lord to rebuke those who offered these requests.

Instead He tells these believers that He will do even more than they have asked.

Surprisingly, the same Jesus who told us to turn the other cheek also teaches to plead with God for justice when we are wronged—and to expect expeditious results (see the story of the widow and the corrupt judge in Luke 18). The Sovereign Lord has promised to effectively accomplish justice in the world for every evil act . . . and then grants permission to passionately and persistently plead with Him to keep this promise.

That's what an imprecatory prayer is—appealing to God to keep his promise to pursue justice on our behalf against the remorseless offenders in our lives—while we are pursuing, or perhaps have exhausted, the appropriate moral and legal options available to us.

This freedom, however, does not come without a serious warning. Pleading with God for retribution is a dangerous thing—dangerous to the one offering the prayer—because God will hold us to the same standard of repentance as our remorseless offenders. So this is not a process that we should enter into lightly or apart from ruthless self-examination.

However, as we pray for the vindication that God has promised, our concerns about that unpaid debt (which can range from mere grudges to consuming obsessions) gradually diminish. Confident that God is able to accomplish the perfect justice that we cannot, we are free to explore the possibility of forgiving those who have hurt us without conscience and to finally emotionally release the offender—and every-thing he owes us—into the discerning and disciplinary hands of God.

———

LET'S FACE IT . . . THERE ARE JUST SOME PASSAGES IN THE BIBLE that you don't hear a lot of sermons based upon. For example, the story of the Levite's concubine (Judg. 19-20), the predicted behavior of the "the most gentle and sensitive" during a barbarous siege (Deut. 28:53-57), or the brutal violations of Dinah and Tamar—and subsequent retal-iation by their brothers (Gen. 34; 2 Sam. 13).

Right up there with these generally-avoided devotional readings are the imprecatory psalms, or as we have called them, The Psalms of Rage. Here are a few of the harsher things that David requests of God against his remorseless enemies . . .

> *Strike them with terror, O LORD; let the nations know they are but men.*
>
> —*Psalm 9:20*

> *Let death take my enemies by surprise; let them go down alive to the grave, for evil finds lodging among them.*
>
> —*Psalm 55:15*

> *Charge them with crime upon crime; do not let them share in your salvation. May they be blotted out of the book of life and not be listed with the right-eous.*
>
> —*Psalm 69:27-28*

Again, I believe David was writing these things to show us his heart as he responded to and reflected upon the evil he encountered in his life.

Perhaps David was thinking of Saul when he wrote, "In his arro-gance, the wicked man hunts down the weak, who are caught in the schemes he devises" (Ps. 10:2); or Nabal when he wrote, "O LORD, the God who avenges, O God who avenges, shine forth. Rise up, O Judge of the earth; pay back to the proud what they deserve. How long will the wicked, O LORD, how long will the wicked be jubilant? They pour out arrogant words; all the evildoers are full of boasting. They crush your people, O LORD; they oppress your inheritance . . . They say, 'The LORD does not see; the God of Jacob pays no heed.'" (Ps. 94:1-5, 7); or Absalom's attempted coup and Shimei's insults when he wrote, "Because of all my enemies, I am the utter contempt of my neighbors; I am a dread to my friends—those who see me on the street flee from me. I am forgotten by them as though I were dead; I have become like broken pottery. For I hear the slander of many; there is terror on every side; they conspire against me and plot to take my life . . . Let me not be put to shame, O LORD, for I have cried out to you; but let the wicked be put to shame and lie silent in the grave. Let their lying lips be silenced, for with pride and contempt they speak arrogantly against the righteous. (Ps. 31:11-13, 17-18).

But because there is no directly recorded response from God to these strongly-worded prayers, Christians have been at a bit of a loss as to how to interpret them. Are they examples of conversations with the Lord that should be avoided or, in some way, imitated? The application models of the imprecatory psalms have generally fallen into six categories.

[Richard J. Vincent has done an excellent job articulating these views and their sources, and so I acknowledge my debt to him for the following summary.]

View 1. They're just plain sinful.

According to this view, the imprecatory psalms are the carnal and vindictive ravings of a man on the precipice of insanity. We always knew King David had a bit of a temper, and these prayers—if you can even call them that—resolve all doubt about the monarch's need for an anger-management class. As such, these prayers are examples of sinful expressions that should be avoided at all costs by the Christian.

View 2. David is just exaggerating—he doesn't really mean all of this.

This view lets David off the hook. The king doesn't really feel this angry toward his enemies; he's just using a bit of poetic license here in order to shock his readers. The people he's talking about have done some very bad things, and David wants his readers to know how bad by the hyperbolic pronouncements of judgment upon them. Whereas

David, as a divinely-inspired writer of the Scriptures, he is given such license—but not so for the common man. These prayers are simply yellow-highlighted descriptions of the consequences of sin—and thus, Christians should still not consider these acceptable forms of petition.

View 3. David is just predicting what will eventually happen to evildoers—he doesn't really expect this sort of thing to happen in his lifetime.

Like the prophets, according to this view, David is simply describing the eventual fate of the remorseless wicked. In poetic terms, this is what the final judgment will be like for those who have taken the king, and God, lightly. But again, this is a prophecy of doom for the distant future—not a temporal occurrence by any means.

View 4. David was "under the law," and now we're "under grace"— What was acceptable for him in Old Testament times does not apply to us since Jesus has come as the "fulfillment of the Law." So David's request for judgment does not apply to us. That sort of thinking belongs to a different age in God's dealings with people.

View 5. In addition to the law/grace argument, we now have more of God's revelation, specifically the teachings of Jesus, to show that these "Psalms of Rage" are inappropriate for the Christian. Jesus often taught "you have heard it said, but now I say to you . . ." And so, the argument goes, the teaching of Jesus about loving our enemies, and openly blessing them (and not cursing) negates these psalms as appropriate for the follower of Christ.

View 6. "The Psalms of Rage" are appropriate for the Christian to pray, but only if God's honor is clearly at stake. The types of rampant wickedness that defames God must certainly be stopped—not only that wickedness might be deterred, but so that all forms of blasphemy is halted. There are limits, therefore, to when the Christian can legitimately offer these prayers: the requests must be based on God's righteousness, not because of our bruised egos—and they must only be offered as a defense of God's glory.

To this last view, I would offer an addendum.

To mess with someone who belongs to God is to mess with God. I think this sentiment is brought out when Jesus, who is glorified and in heaven, asks Saul the religious terrorist, a question. Saul is on his way to Damascus to arrest and probably kill Christians, when Jesus throws him off his horse and demands to know "Why are you persecuting *me?*" (emphasis added). When Jesus rebukes the "goats" at the final judgment, He says, in essence, "The evils of omission you committed against the least of these my brethren, you committed against me." So, I don't think we need to analyze every act of evil to see if God's honor is at stake. God takes it personally when someone He loves is wronged.

So, there are the different views. Without a direct response from God, we're stuck as to how to interpret these harsh prayers of David. If only we could hear both sides of the conversation, then the interpretation would be clear. If these prayers provoked a harsh rebuke from the Lord, then the answer would be clear—we should have nothing to do with these types of prayers.

If only other people in the Bible had offered these types of prayers, and were not rebuked, but supported by God, then we'd be closer to seeing a legitimate application of the similar psalms.

And better yet, if some of these people were in the New Testament, and also got an affirmative response from God, then all questions about being "under the law or under grace" or having a lack of complete revelation would be silenced.

And best of all, if some of these people were already in heaven, glorified and freed from the presence of all sin, and *still* offered these prayers, and *still* got an "I'll make it happen" response from God, then we would have to concede that it's legitimate for Christians today, under certain circumstances, to plead with God to accomplish justice on their behalf in this manner.

Well, we do have other people the Bible who offered imprecatory prayers like David, and they did get an immediate and positive response from God. Some of them were in the Old Testament, and some were in the New Testament—and some of those believers were glorified, freed-from-sin saints in heaven.

Let's take a look at these people who had been wronged and see what we can learn from their prayerful examples—and God's response to them.

God responds to Jeremiah

The prophet Elijah was given fire from heaven against the prophets of Baal. The prophet Isaiah was given spectacular visions of Christ before the foundations of the world. The prophet Elisha was given the power to raise the dead son of a widow and gave him back to his mother.

In contrast, the prophet Jeremiah was given a belt of dripping, beat-up cloth—and told by God to use it as an object lesson.

Jeremiah was also told by God never to marry and raise a family because it would only increase his grief when Judah's judgment finally came. His writings were cut to pieces and burned in the king's court as a sign of contempt for the prophet. His message was one of impending, inevitable doom: repentance may hold off God's temporal justice for a while, but you might as well pack your bags, because the Babylonians are coming.

And for speaking the truth in love, Jeremiah's fellow Judeans beat him up, threw him into a makeshift prison, and eventually lowered him into an old well with nothing but mud on the bottom—presumably to die. Not only did Jeremiah accurately predict the disastrous fall of Judah, but he personally witnessed its demise. And he recorded his feelings about the event in a funeral dirge we know as the Book of Lamentations.

No wonder Jeremiah is called the weeping prophet.

As the psalms are a window into David's soul, we are also given many insights into Jeremiah's heart and feelings. Personality-wise, he tended to be melancholy. And all the abuse heaped upon him by his countrymen did not make things any better for him. He reached a point where he had finally had enough of those who were attempting to discredit him and thus nullify his prophetic message from the Lord.

> They said, "Come, let's make plans against
> Jeremiah; for the teaching of the law by the priest will
> not be lost, nor will counsel from the wise, nor the
> word from the prophets. So come, let's attack him with
> our tongues and pay no attention to anything he says."
>
> Listen to me, O LORD; hear what my accusers
> are saying!
>
> Should good be repaid with evil? Yet they have
> dug a pit for me. Remember that I stood before you

and spoke in their behalf to turn your wrath away from them.

So give their children over to famine; hand them over to the power of the sword. Let their wives be made childless and widows; let their men be put to death, their young men slain by the sword in battle.

Let a cry be heard from their houses when you suddenly bring invaders against them, for they have dug a pit to capture me and have hidden snares for my feet.

But you know, O LORD, all their plots to kill me.

Do not forgive their crimes or blot out their sins from your sight. Let them be overthrown before you; deal with them in the time of your anger.
—Jeremiah 18:18-23

At other times, Jeremiah made similar requests . . .

But, O LORD Almighty, you who judge righteously and test the heart and mind, let me see your vengeance upon them, for to you I have committed my cause.
—Jeremiah 11:20

O LORD Almighty, you who examine the righteous and probe the heart and mind, let me see your vengeance upon them, for to you I have committed my cause.
—Jeremiah 20:12

Unlike similar imprecatory psalms, we are fortunate to have an immediate response from God to Jeremiah's cries for retribution. While it is true that to attack Jeremiah's message was to attack God, these cries of Jeremiah are quite personal and to the point. He wants the people who have hurt him to pay for their relentlessly damaging behavior.

In God's immediate response to Jeremiah, there is not even a hint of rebuke for the prophet. Instead, the Lord promises that he will do even more than the prophet has requested.

> *"'In this place I will ruin the plans of Judah and Jerusalem. I will make them fall by the sword before their enemies, at the hands of those who seek their lives, and I will give their carcasses as food to the birds of the air and the beasts of the earth. I will devastate this city and make it an object of scorn; all who pass by will be appalled and will scoff because of all its wounds. . . .'"*
>
> —Jeremiah 19:7-8

Apparently the Lord desired just retribution for the evil deeds of these people even more than the prophet did.

God responds to Habakkuk

Another Old Testament prophet who had finally had enough of evil people and their arrogance was Habakkuk. Jeremiah and Habakkuk were contemporaries and probably dealt with the same wanton religious leaders. Habakkuk was another saint who passionately asked God for retribution and accountability.

> *How long, O LORD, must I call for help, but you do not listen?*
>
> *Or cry out to you, "Violence!" but you do not save?*
>
> *Why do you make me look at injustice? Why do you tolerate wrong?*
>
> *Destruction and violence are before me; there is strife, and conflict abounds.*
>
> *Therefore the law is paralyzed, and justice never prevails.*
>
> *The wicked hem in the righteous, so that justice is perverted.*
>
> —Habakkuk 1:2-3

Like Jeremiah, we have an immediate response to Habakkuk's prayer for retribution, but the answer takes the prophet by surprise.

> *"Look at the nations and watch—and be utterly amazed.*

For I am going to do something in your days that you would not believe, even if you were told.

I am raising up the Babylonians, that ruthless and impetuous people, who sweep across the whole earth to seize dwelling places not their own.

They are a feared and dreaded people; they are a law to themselves and promote their own honor.

Their horses are swifter than leopards, fiercer than wolves at dusk.

Their cavalry gallops headlong; their horsemen come from afar.

They fly like a vulture swooping to devour; they all come bent on violence.

Their hordes advance like a desert wind and gather prisoners like sand.

They deride kings and scoff at rulers.

They laugh at all fortified cities; they build earth-en ramps and capture them.

Then they sweep past like the wind and go on—guilty men, whose own strength is their god."

— *Habakkuk 1:5-11*

(Habakkuk's response)

O LORD, are you not from everlasting? My God, my Holy One, we will not die.

O LORD, you have appointed them to execute judgment; O Rock, you have ordained them to punish.

Your eyes are too pure to look on evil; you cannot tolerate wrong.

Why then do you tolerate the treacherous? Why are you silent while the wicked swallow up those more righteous than themselves?

— *Habakkuk 1:12-13*

Like Jeremiah, the Lord was willing to do more for Habakkuk than the prophet asked. But in this case, the Lord's actions seemed too extreme, even to the exasperated prophet. It was as if Habakkuk was saying, "Whoa, you need to do something, but this is too much. How can you eradicate evil with an even greater evil? The players you're bringing in are far worse than the players you're taking out."

But the Lord's answer is the same. When their cup is full (that of the wicked Babylonians), then they too will be expelled from the land—by whatever superpower happens to be available. History tells us that it was the Medes and the Persians.

One of the underlying messages of God's response to Habakkuk is that people and nations can only serve one of two roles in the Kingdom of God—they're either pawns or servants. The Babylonians, specifically Nebuchadnezzar, was used by God to purge Israel of its idolatry and to provide a crucible for the magnificent ministry and visions of Daniel. When Nebuchanezzer's head got too big, the Lord took his sanity away in the twinkling of an eye—and then, seven years later, gave it back to him just as quickly.

Though the fools in our lives may think they're getting away with something, in truth, the Lord is simply using them in ways that would surprise even them. And some of them, when they do discover that they were simply used as pawns, will tell the Lord that He wouldn't have been successful without them.

Even in the presence of God, their insolence will be impenetrable.

Unrest in heaven

> When he opened the fifth seal, I saw under the altar the souls of those who had been slain because of the word of God and the testimony they had maintained. They called out in a loud voice, "How long, Sovereign Lord, holy and true, until you judge the inhabitants of the earth and avenge our blood?" Then each of them was given a white robe, and they were told to wait a little longer, until the number of their fellow servants and brothers who were to be killed as they had been was completed.
>
> —Revelation 6:9-11

Regardless of your view of the last days, there's something about these saints under the altar that hits us as out of the ordinary. In fact, the famous atheistic philosopher, Nietzsche, commented that these saints prove that Christianity isn't all forgiveness and light. Let's look at the facts . . .

These "souls" are followers of Christ whose lives have been taken from them because of their identification with Christ. Some have inferred that these saints represent all Christians, in an allegorical sense, who have given up their lives to follow Jesus. In any case, these saints had been killed in the line of duty. It's sobering to note that more Christians around the world have died for their faith in the last century than in all of Christian history.

As Stephen, the first Christian martyr, was being executed, perhaps as the last stones were being hurled at him, he cried out to God and said "Lord, do not hold this sin against them." (Acts 7:60). The martyred saints of Revelation 6 say nothing of the sort; in fact, they ask God *how long* it's going to be before He avenges their spilled blood. The words translated "revenge" and "vengeance" in Romans 12:19 and Hebrews 10:30 have the same root as the word translated "avenge" here in Revelation 6:10.

Keep in mind, these are glorified saints. They have been freed, not only from the penalty of sin, but also from the presence of sin, in their very beings. Whatever you believe about the possibility of sinless perfection during our time on earth, by the grace of God, these heavenly saints had attained such a state. Of course, in other cases, when we are interpreting the statements of certain biblical characters, you have to keep in mind that some of them are struggling with the old sinful nature. Not so here; we can safely assume that there's nothing sinful in these saints' request for divine revenge.

Let's look at their prayer. First, they acknowledge God as their Sovereign Lord—not just "Lord"—but *Sovereign* Lord. By using this title, they acknowledge their unconditional acquiescence to sovereign will. Whatever He decrees, they will accept—without question. They acknowledge that their Sovereign Lord is holy and true. Thus, he cannot allow sin to go unanswered forever, and He will unquestionably do whatever it is He has promised to do.

The question of whether or not those who took their lives will be held accountable does not come up. There is no question in the minds of these saints that God is *going* to avenge them—they just want to know *how long* they're going to have to wait. This restlessness seems out of place for heaven . . . but there it is, all the same.

In response to their request, each is given a white robe. This is often interpreted as a symbol of their righteousness in Christ and God's affirmation. So even before the time of their vindication is at hand, they are given something to comfort them.

After receiving this gift, they are told that they are going to have to wait . . . not indefinitely, but just a little longer. And they are given a reason for the delay: they must wait until the "full number" of believers killed for their faith (in God's sovereign plan) is completed. And this plan had to run its full course before the time of retribution would come.

These glorified saints asked a two-worded question that was common among many of the biblical saints, and thousands of frustrated saints today . . . *how long?*

David laments in "How long must your servant wait? When will you punish my persecutors?" (Ps. 119:84). Habakkuk cries out, "How long, O LORD, must I call for help, but you do not listen? Or cry out to you, 'Violence!' but you do not save?" (Hab. 1:2). Sometimes these believers lose a little patience and get a little edgy . . . as when David asks the Lord, "How long will you defend the unjust and show partiality to the wicked?" (Ps. 82:2).

A contemporary believer might ask God, "If I cannot take my own revenge, then *how long* do I have to wait until you act? *How long* until you keep your promise of vindication and retribution? *How long* do I have to wait so I can have some sort of idea of when you're going to take some action?"

The following chapter will talk about what to do when the feelings of "how long until God does something" come up when we're waiting for God to fulfill His promise. In fact, it will outline all the steps you should take when you encounter remorseless evil.

So, if you feel that it's appropriate to move forward, then please continue on. However, you are about to enter a very dangerous area of reflection and action where you might discover things about yourself that may make you very uncomfortable. In our biblical response to evil, we may very well discover its presence in our own hearts—and if so, we must deal with it accordingly.

7 Preparing Our Hearts, Moving Forward

Under certain circumstances, Christians are invited to follow the example of the imprecatory prayers of struggling saints in the Bible in order to increase their emotional confidence in God's perfect justice —thus providing a sense of acknowledgment, vindication, and closure that they cannot accomplish on their own.

Do you rent or own responsibility?

Have you ever filled out an application for a loan and seen a question that asks: "Do you own or rent your home?"

We all know why the lender asks this question. Owning or renting a house doesn't make you a better person, but it seems to make you a better risk — at least as far as bankers are concerned.

In some neighborhoods, you can go down a street and kind of tell who owns their houses, and who's just paying the rent. Renters, while they may be neat and responsible, just don't have as much at stake when it comes to the building that they live in. If there's a problem, many don't seek to fix it themselves, they just call the landlord. Some renters are not required to maintain their property at all. Again, they just depend on the owner of the building. Some renters consider this their privilege, because, when all is said and done, they have nothing to show for the thousands of dollars they shell out year after year.

1

The homeowner, on the other hand, is completely responsible for the maintenance and upkeep of his property. There's no landlord to call if the lawn needs mowing, the washer is banging, or the roof needs to be replaced. However, at the end of a certain length of time (usually the duration of a mortgage), the homeowner has something to show for his efforts. So he is motivated to keep up his investment.

Now, try to imagine filling out a survey that's trying to determine your level of spiritual maturity. And you come across the question: "Do you rent or own a sense of personal responsibility?"

As children progress in their spiritual development, in a sense they "rent" the faith of their parents. For children, this is very natural, and it's a good thing. In many Christian homes, these children attend Sunday school and mid-week programs, they hear their Moms and Dads pray at the dinner table, and, if they're lucky, they observe their parents' faith in action. They hear their Moms and Dads talk about trusting God, sharing their faith, and the importance of applying the Scriptures to their lives. And then these little observers step back and watch to see how their parents react when conflicts arise, an unexpected crisis occurs, or a neighbor loses his job. Even if all does not go perfectly, and these Christian parents do not respond ideally, these kids begin to understand that faith in Christ is a meaningful thing. In a sense, they say to themselves "I believe in Jesus because my parents do . . . because they must know what they're talking about."

Then there comes a magical moment when a maturing child no longer believes just because his or her parents believe. At this mysterious intersection between childhood and adulthood, this person realizes that he or she has all the mental, emotional, and spiritual resources needed to accept full liability for his or her own growth in Christ . . . and this person accepts that obligation. This is the moment of faith ownership—when an individual no longer "rents the faith of others" but accepts, or "owns," full responsibility for who she is in Christ—and consequently, for all of this individual's thoughts, words, decisions, and actions.

THE STORY OF THE WOMAN AT THE WELL IN JOHN 4 is an excellent biblical illustration of one person who went from "renting" her beliefs from a surrounding culture, to "owning" her faith in such a way that it changed her life in a dramatic manner. And, this not only happened to the woman in this story, but also to those in her community who heard her testimony and then had their own "faith-ownership" experience.

In this story, Jesus and his disciples are traveling through Samaria on their way to Galilee. Of course, most Israelites avoided Samaria by taking a longer, harder route by traveling on the east side of the Jordan River. This was because, for centuries, the Israelites had considered the Samaritans traitors and half-breeds. The Samaritans were descendants of Israelites who had intermarried with their Babylonian captors. Because of this frequent intermarriage, the Israelites considered the Samaritans as unclean, and so would have nothing to do with them. At this well, Jesus engaged in a discussion with a Samaritan woman who apparently had quite a bit of experience with repeated intermarriage.

The woman was surprised that this Jewish man would even talk to her, much less ask her for a drink. Not only did Israelites refuse to speak with Samaritans, but Jewish men had no business addressing a woman. In addition, she probably had a tainted reputation even amongst her fellow Samaritans. As we learn later in the story, she had had five husbands, and she was not married to the man with whom she was currently living. This might explain why she was getting water at such an unusual time of the day—she did not go down when the other women usually went (around dawn), because they probably excluded her from their conversations and effectively pushed her away.

During her conversation with Jesus, the woman constantly referred to her people's spiritual heritage . . . and the Lord kept poking holes in her "rented" beliefs. According to Jesus, worship wasn't a matter of religious heritage, prime religious real estate (namely Jerusalem), or marital status. God wanted people who would worship Him in spirit and in truth. And to do this, individuals had to enter into a reconciled relationship with God through the atoning work of the Messiah that He sent—in fact, the very person with whom she was speaking.

The biblical record offers no details about the conversion of the Samaritan woman—but we can tell by her actions that she had undergone some sort of dramatic transformation. When the disciples returned, she took off, leaving behind a very valuable item . . . her water jar. Since she had discovered the source of living water, her purely physical needs did not seem to take on the same significance they once did. She ran back to her community, to the very people who were probably shunning her, to tell them about Jesus. At this point, we can be fairly certain that she had placed her trust in Christ. Even so, she invites the people in her town to come to their own faith-related conclusions by asking them the question, "Could this be the Christ?"

After inviting Jesus to their town, and listening to him teach, many of them became believers. Prior to that, several others became Christians on the sole testimony of the Samaritan woman. However, after they had experienced Jesus for themselves, they said an interesting thing to the person who introduced them to Jesus.

They said to the woman, "We no longer believe just because of what you said; now we have heard for ourselves, and we know that this man really is the Savior of the world." They had abandoned the "rented" faith of their ancestors, and now were trusting Christ because of their own experience with Him.

As we talked about earlier, many Christians experience a "magical moment" in their lives where they cross the line of faith-rental to faith-ownership. They no longer say, "Well, if I'm not growing spiritually, it's my pastor's fault, or my spouse's fault, or it's the fault of all those people who make so many demands on my time." They stop saying, "I believe in these doctrines because they're in my church's statement of faith, and it's what I'm supposed to believe." Instead, they cling to the essentials of the faith, the doctrines of historic Christianity, because they have wrestled with these teachings, and found them to be true.

I HAD ONE OF THESE TRANSITIONAL EXPERIENCES in middle school that really brought this point home to me. It was the first day of sixth grade, and I had been assigned to my first male teacher. This mysterious man had a reputation for being tough and unpredictable in the classroom.

To say the least, I was terrified of being in this guy's class. As the first day began, he seemed pleasant enough, but I was just waiting for the other shoe to drop.

Later in the week, it did. He gave us a choice that I had never faced as an elementary student. In his first option, we could learn about decimals in the traditional way . . . that is, he would show us how to solve certain problems, and then we'd wrestle with twenty to thirty math exercises to do as homework. As the teacher, he would set the pace.

Or, option two, we could sign a contract that said we'd agree to learn about decimals on our own—to go as fast or slow as we wanted, with the guarantee that the teacher would be there to help us if we got stuck.

All of us chose option two.

As soon as I signed that contract, it suddenly hit me that I was now fully responsible for what I learned and what I needed to learn. And not just about decimals, but everything. This responsibility no longer rested with my teachers. They may present material, but it was up to me to absorb it—no matter how talented or compelling they were. If I wanted to know something beyond what they were presenting, it was up to me to do the exploration. If I didn't have the tools that I needed, there were people out there who could help me get what I needed—but I had to ask. If I didn't know something that I needed or wanted to know, I simply no longer had anyone to blame but myself. And that felt great.

When I became a Christian several years later, that principle stuck with me. As an adult, no one was going to be responsible for my spiritual growth. If I was going to mature in Christ, it was going to be up to me. Granted, I was going to be utterly dependent on the spiritual gifts of others in order to grow in my faith. But I wasn't to going sit around waiting for these people to come to me—I would need to seek them out.

Owning, not renting, personal responsibility for our own thoughts, words, and actions—good and bad—must happen before we even think about approaching God regarding the remorseless people in our lives.

No double standard . . .

It doesn't matter if a person jumps into the deep end of a pool feet first, head first, or doing a belly flop—the law of gravity is going to kick in and pull that person into the water. Apart from God's supernatural intervention, the law of gravity is immutable—that is, it's unchanging, and applies in the same way to everybody. No matter how you jump off the end of the diving board, you're going to end up in the water.

God also has certain laws when it comes to His response to specific human behaviors. Granted, He is powerful enough to supernaturally intervene and make an exception—but in regard to the following behavioral law, there seems to be no biblical basis for God ever making an exception.

And it's not a surprising law—no one's ever going to slap themselves on the head and say, "Oh, I didn't know that." Not only is this behavioral law repeated extensively and clearly in the Scriptures, one could argue that this law is intuitively the most easily discerned.

Here it is, plainly stated . . .

> *"In the same way you judge others, you will be judged, and with the measure you use, it will be measured to you. Why do you look at the speck of sawdust in your brother's eye and pay no attention to the plank in your own eye? How can you say to your brother, 'Let me take the speck out of your eye,' when all the time there is a plank in your own eye? You hypocrite, first take the plank out of your own eye, and then you will see clearly to remove the speck from your brother's eye."*
> —Matthew 7:2-5

Christians have argued for centuries what it means "to not judge." Paul clearly tells us we are to judge ourselves within the church (1 Cor. 5:12), and the whole basis of Jesus' outline for church discipline assumes that we will judge some behavior as ungodly and unacceptable.

The context of Matthew 7 implies that we are not to label behavior as unacceptable until we have undergone our own ruthless self-examination—and put our own quirks, idiosyncrasies, and self-justified actions under the same microscope that God will use to judge others. That's frightening.

The goal of this introspection is not to get us to the point of saying that the remorseless behavior of others doesn't matter, because, in the end, we're all just sinners anyway. The goal, according to Jesus, *is the ability to see clearly* so that we can effectively confront the sins of others. The implication of Matthew 7:5 is that we should be able to eventually get to that point.

So how is this self-examination best accomplished?

Look again at Matthew 7:2—"For in the same way you judge others, you will be judged, and with the measure you use, it will be measured to you." Simply apply to yourself the same standards of accountability you would require of someone who had offended you and genuinely wanted to be reconciled with you. Ask yourself . . .

Do I acknowledge that my behavior in this matter dishonored God?

Do I take full responsibility for the damaging consequences of that behavior?

What God-honoring actions am I going to take to replace that unacceptable behavior—whether it was a one-time event or pattern of disobedience?

Failing in any of these, do I desire reconciliation enough to ask for mercy?

Here's another scary question to consider . . . who might be reading this book with you in mind? If they were to go through these questions with you, how would you respond?

[Again, this calls for much wisdom and discernment—the shrewdly remorseless in this world are constantly looking for other people to take responsibility for their thoughts, words, decisions, and actions. So, if you are confronted in this way, be sure it's legitimate. As ruthlessly as you must accept responsibility for your own thoughts, words, and deeds—you must be just as passionate for rejecting responsibility for the thoughts, words, and deeds of others. Be careful when self-examination starts leading to thoughts of self-rejection.]

Forgiving ourselves—facing the vortex

What about those who cannot seem to forgive themselves? Many in this predicament often find they can easily forgive others, sometimes too quickly, at even the slightest hint of repentance. But they cannot apply the same grace to themselves that they apply to others.

Despite its frequent anti-faith bias, the *Star Trek Next Generation* series often provided good story lines. In one such episode, Captain Picard is confronted with a representation of himself that came from six hours in the future. The future Picard is disoriented, because for him, time is a mirror image of reality, and he cannot make out his surroundings, or communicate with his present self.

The context of this encounter is the imminent destruction of the Enterprise as it's being sucked into a black hole of sorts. Even with the engines at maximum warp, the captain cannot pull the ship out of the vice-like grip of this vortex. Probes sent into the middle of the vortex are immediately destroyed, and so the same fate clearly awaits the ship and its crew. As the two time dimensions come closer to one another, the future Picard seems dead-set on leaving the ship, which seems contrary to what the present Picard would do. Why would any worthy captain, especially one like Captain Picard, abandon ship in the face of imminent danger, leaving his crew behind?

The story line reveals that the future Picard believes that there is some sort of intelligence behind the vortex who only wants him—and if he sacrifices himself, then the ship and the rest of the crew will be spared. The present Picard has reservations about this course of action and summarily disables the future representation of himself. The present Picard then surprises the crew and tells the pilot to direct the ship at warp speed directly into the sucking tentacles of the vortex.

Of course, the loyal crew obeys his orders, and the ship heads straight into the vortex . . . and safely comes out the other side.

All this by way of analogy: some of us may wrestle with versions of ourselves, versions of ourselves that we can't forgive—and that makes us very uncomfortable.

Quite possibly, those who struggle with forgiving themselves may have never really come to terms with the depth and the damage of their sin—that is, they have not fully acknowledged the pain they've caused themselves and others.

This path, and no other, is the road to God's forgiveness—and ultimately self-forgiveness. There is nothing but grace for those who fully acknowledge their sin. And again, this means more than just saying you're sorry and asking for forgiveness—it means plunging into the vortex of the malicious motives behind what you can't forgive in yourself—and then experiencing the cleansing forgiveness of God.

It's not easy; in fact, it's downright terrifying—but the result will be a contrite heart that God promises He will not despise. And the self-forgiveness that has seemed so elusive may just suddenly show up at your doorstep.

Have you done everything you can do?

After the ruthless self-examination, you must ask yourself if all the appropriate steps to attaining appropriate earthly justice have been taken. In the realm of criminal activity, that would include the existing court systems. No matter how bloated and ineffective they may seem to you, the government is God's ministering arm of justice (Rom. 13:4) and must be given due respect. The same is true of appropriate civil cases, where existing mediation services have proven ineffective — and human justice remains outstanding.

If the offense is committed by a Christian—or someone who has associated himself with a local congregation, and the offense is clearly a violation of some biblical standard, then the process of church discipline outlined in Matthew 18 must be initiated by the offended party. The first step is private confrontation—but there is grace here if taking such a step would put the victim in harm's way. Private confrontation must first be safe and responsible if it is to ever be effective—so this first step calls for prudence. If private confrontation fails to produce an appropriate penitent response (that is, the acknowledgment of the specific sin, the acceptance of personal responsibility for that particular action, and an action plan to replace the offensive behavior with a pattern of behavior that honors God), then we are to take two or three witnesses and continue the confrontation. If that fails, then the person is to be taken to the church leadership—and barring the appropriate penitent response—is to then be "treated as an unbeliever"—that is, a remorseless individual who has rejected the grace of God.

And the sad truth is, as we pointed out earlier, sometimes earthly justice or effective church discipline is unattainable—because of a lack of evidence (that might have even been destroyed by the offender), a lack of interest or even corruption on the part of judicial prosecutors or church leadership, savvy defense lawyers who convinced a jury to believe something that wasn't true, or a good-ol'-boy network in the congregation that knows how to sweep certain embarrassing incidents under the church carpet (the color of which almost caused a church split).

The failure to receive earthly justice—or the improbable prospect that earthly justice will ever be attained—is probably the number one motive for deeply-pained human beings to pursue revenge on their own behalf. The emotional disequilibrium that justice-denied produces is a powerful driving force for many who seek to balance the scales on their own.

But this particular step must end here; once you have done all you can, morally and legally speaking, then the prayer of retribution is the only God-honoring action you can take. Besides, it is the only emotionally-satisfying option available to you. Seeking gratification beyond that which you may have been denied from the established systems of accountability will put you on the same plane, if not a lower one, than the remorseless individual who seems to be getting away with something—at your expense.

Keeping it private . . .

"I JUST WANT YOU TO KNOW that I'm praying for your death."

Don's quiet wife was usually not so "in-his-face" when she was upset. This was their first "date" without the kids in three months—maybe he should have taken her to some place a little classier than Burger Bob's.

"Yeah, I'm reading this book about praying for revenge, and I'm sick of waiting for you to change. You won't clean up after yourself, you do nothing around the house, you don't appreciate anything I do, and I'm constantly repeating myself to you!"

"What did you say?"

"See? See that? So, yeah, I wish you were dead. A heart attack would be fine, but if you got hit by some sort of delivery truck, that would probably come with a nice settlement."

Telling someone that you're praying for retribution against him or her is itself a form of forbidden revenge. You're trying to create in that person a sense of dread—and if he truly is remorseless he's not going to be convinced that he's done anything to provoke God's discipline. So you end up just looking like a fool . . . you'll just be accused of over-reacting again. He'll probably just repeat your words to others, and the ol' offender/victim switch will take place.

The imprecatory prayer for justice and retribution must only occur in the private sanctuary of prayer—and never, ever leave that place.

Don't tell anyone you're doing it. (With the possible exception of a mature friend or competent counselor who is helping you through this process. You must be absolutely convinced, however, that this person will keep this confidential.) No one needs to know, and it will never be anyone's business to know.

Offering up the prayer of retribution

There are times in the Christian's life when it's appropriate to offer up prayers similar to the imprecatory petitions of David, Jeremiah, Habakkuk, and the saints of Revelation 6. But the qualifier of "appropriate" has always been there. What conditions must first be met?

1. The Christian who has been hurt by an unrepentant offender must himself come to a state of "blamelessness" — even as Job and David have been described. Blameless is not the same as innocent.

"For all have sinned and fall short of the glory of God" (Romans 3:23). Ironically, the Christian becomes blameless by accepting and then acknowledging blame when it's appropriate. What we desire the offender to do, we must also do in the others areas of our life that may not fully honor God. Again, it is as uncomplicated as "**A, B, C, M**" — **A.** Acknowledging the wrong that was committed; **B.** Bearing the burden for the damage that behavior caused; **C.** Correcting the errant actions by substituting a behavior that will keep us from returning to the foolishness of our past . . . and then appealing for **M**, mercy if these actions prove ineffective, despite our best efforts.

2. All established avenues of secular justice and church discipline, again—when appropriate—must be initiated and, at least, on the way to being fully exhausted. These systems, while sometimes cumbersome and inefficient when it comes to addressing our emotional needs, are absolutely vital when it comes to human accountability and the deterrence of even greater evil. These processes have been established by God to provoke repentance in the hard-hearted—and sometimes they actually succeed in doing so. So they must not be forsaken or taken lightly. They must precede, or at least be set in motion, before any consideration of taking the most serious step of imprecatory prayer.

3. If the first two conditions have been met, and the person who is suffering from the remorseless evil of others does not have the emotional confidence that God will vindicate him or her . . . then the prayer of retribution can be offered in good faith.

Keep in mind that this is not voodoo, or the casting of some witch's spell. Balaam was a corrupt prophet in the Old Testament who was called upon by a foreign king to openly curse Israel. He was eventually stopped by his talking donkey — with whom Balaam had an extensive conversation. Balaam got a lot of things wrong, but he certainly spoke the truth when he said, "How can I curse those whom God has not cursed? How can I denounce those whom the LORD has not denounced?" (Num. 23:8).

God knows the hidden thoughts and motivations of the person who has hurt you. If the person is not guilty of the things you accuse him of (in your prayer)—God knows this and is not going to take the action you've requested. "Like a fluttering sparrow or a darting swallow, an undeserved curse does not come to rest" (Prov. 26:2).

If the person is guilty—perhaps even more than you realize—then God is going to fulfill his promise, and act accordingly in this person's life . . . but only in accordance with His often-mysterious, but utterly sovereign plans for the tens, hundreds, and even thousands of people who are connected to your life in some way.

All prayers, especially prayers for vindication, pass through the divine filter of the Holy Spirit. "In the same way, the Spirit helps us in our weakness. We do not know what we ought to pray for, but the Spirit himself intercedes for us with groans that words cannot express" (Rom. 8:26). So if you've sufficiently dealt with the sins you clearly know about, and you've taken every possible moral and legal step to address the problem—and the offender is still remorseless—then let the prayerful floodgates loose. Tell the Lord exactly how you feel and what you want to see happen—and let Him sort it all out.

Again, all this must only take place in the private sanctuary of prayer where no one, even the devil, can hear what you're saying. Talk about this with no one, *especially* the person you're praying about. (Again, the possible exception to this might include sharing this with a trusted friend or competent counselor who is helping you through the process—someone you are absolutely certain will keep this confidential.) The words you speak in public, even to the offender, must be seasoned with grace and cordiality.

Letting others know that you're doing this—perhaps with the hope that it will get around to the offender—is itself a form of forbidden revenge and will only come around to bite you back.

So after you've done all that the Scriptures have allowed you to do (and make no mistake—it's a lot of painstaking work; there's nothing passive about it)—what then are we commanded to do?

We are to wait . . . specifically, to wait on the Lord.

In our fast-paced, take-life-by-the-throat culture, *waiting* is usually frowned upon. I was in a bookstore recently when the man ahead of me in line mentioned to the cashier that people spend over six years of their lives waiting in line—and he wanted her to know just how much of that six years she had taken up.

Even Dr. Seuss liked to take a poke or two at "waiting." In his book, *Oh The Places You'll Go*, he describes "a most useless place" he calls "The Waiting Place." What Dr. Seuss is making fun of here, very effectively I might add, is the type of passive attitude that some people have who are simply waiting for life to happen to them. They are the folks who just can't seem to get a break — so they spend their lives waiting around for one. Of all the great advice that could be given to young adults just venturing out into the world, this is some of the best.

Waiting on the Lord, however, is nothing like "The Waiting Place" of Dr. Seuss' rich imagination. Consider the beautiful poetic language in which the sweet and comforting presence of the Lord is described in a time of waiting.

> *The LORD is a God of justice. Blessed are all who wait for him!*
>
> *—Isaiah 30:18b*

> *In the morning, O LORD, you hear my voice; in the morning I lay my requests before you and wait in expectation.*
>
> *—Psalm 5:3*

> *Wait for the LORD; be strong and take heart and wait for the LORD.*
>
> *—Psalm 27:14*

> *We wait in hope for the LORD; he is our help and our shield.*
>
> *—Psalm 33:20*

> *I wait for you, O LORD; you will answer, O Lord my God.*
>
> *—Psalm 38:15*

> *I waited patiently for the LORD; he turned to me and heard my cry.*
>
> *—Psalm 40:1*

> *I wait for your salvation, O LORD, and I follow your commands.*
>
> *—Psalm 119:166*

I wait for the LORD, *my soul waits, and in his*
word I put my hope.

—*Psalm 130:5*

My soul waits for the Lord more than watchmen
wait for the morning, more than watchmen wait for
the morning.

—*Psalm 130:6*

It is good to wait quietly for the salvation of the
LORD.

—*Lamentations 3:26*

Since ancient times no one has heard, no ear has
perceived, no eye has seen any God besides you,
who acts on behalf of those who wait for him.

—*Isaiah 64:4*

Waiting seems to be a lot easier in times of peace. But what are we
to do when justice is denied or insufficient—and the wicked gloat and
strut over all that they've gotten away with?

Do we still wait then?

Do not say, "I'll pay you back for this wrong!"
Wait for the LORD, *and he will deliver you.*

—*Proverbs 20:22*

Be still before the LORD *and wait patiently for*
him; do not fret when men succeed in their ways,
when they carry out their wicked schemes.

—*Psalm 37:7*

Wait for the LORD *and keep his way. He will*
exalt you to inherit the land; when the wicked are cut
off, you will see it.

—*Psalm 37:34*

"Therefore wait for me," declares the LORD,
"for the day I will stand up to testify. I have decided
to assemble the nations, to gather the kingdoms and
to pour out my wrath on them—all my fierce anger.

The whole world will be consumed by the fire of my
jealous anger."

—Zephaniah 3:8

Therefore judge nothing before the appointed
time; wait till the Lord comes. He will bring to light
what is hidden in darkness and will expose the
motives of men's hearts. At that time each will
receive his praise from God.

—1 Corinthians 4:5

So, after we have done everything in our power—everything that the laws of the land and the power of the church allows us to do, we are to wait on the Lord.

While you're waiting . . .

What are we to do while we are in the place of prayer and waiting on the Lord?

At the risk of sounding insensitive, do something else.

Resist the temptation to psychoanalyze the situation—for example, trying to figure out why the offender acted in such a way. (Would it really matter if the ultimate reason was that he was teased too much as a child or received poor toilet training?).

Instead, ask yourself "what is the next, most responsible thing I can do?" And if there's nothing else for you to do in this particular matter (besides prayer and waiting on the Lord), do that next, most responsible thing. All the emotional and spiritual energy you would have spent fretting, planning, plotting, implementing, and eventually suffering from, the revenge you are clearly forbidden to pursue can now be directed toward appropriate, healthy, and safe relationships. There are many people in the church who do not have your spiritual gifts, and so there are pockets of need that someone with only your giftedness can fill.

The "Waiting on the Lord Place" is a place of wonder, worship, and a refreshing sense of well-being. There we find rest, refuge, and new realizations. As your confidence in God's willingness to act on your behalf grows, your concerns about past offenses will diminish. And as the truly penitent person embraces new healthy behaviors to replace a previous pattern of sin, so must we redirect our new-found energy in ways that honor God.

What should happen after all this has occurred?

In every biblical prayer of retribution, we can sense a change in attitude in those who offered the prayers. I see it as an ever-increasing confidence in God's willingness to vindicate them and to achieve ultimate justice on their behalf—above and beyond what any human system or process could accomplish.

For example, almost all of the imprecatory psalms end in an expression of worship. As the psalmist prays for retribution, perhaps he begins to realize the terrible and awful fate that awaits the hard-hearted, and he is moved to worship.

> Live, then, and be happy, beloved children of my heart, and never forget that until the day when God shall deign to reveal the future to man, all human wisdom is summed up in these two words —
>
> Wait and hope.
>
> Your friend,
> Edmond Dantes
>
> —*The Count of Monte Cristo*
> by Alexandre Dumas

The last words of the first martyr, Stephen, were "Lord do not hold this sin against them." He has just seen the Son of God standing at the right hand of God, and fully understood the fate of those who were hurling rocks at him and remained impenitent. Because Stephen fully realized the terrifying end of his enemies, he asked for mercy on their behalf. One of the beneficiaries of his prayer was the eventual-apostle Paul, who was holding the coats of Stephen's executioners. Surely Paul (then Saul) heard these final words of this knowledgeable and faithful man, and wondered about the source of such improbable compassion.

After Habakkuk complained to God, asking for justice, the Lord responded in ways he could hardly comprehend. After resigning himself to God's sovereignty, the prophet speaks these words of worship: "Though the fig tree does not bud and there are no grapes on the vines, though the olive crop fails and the fields produce no food, though there are no sheep in the pen and no cattle in the stalls, yet I will rejoice in the Lord, I will be joyful in God my Savior" (Hab. 3:17-18).

After God responded to Jeremiah's prayers with the heavy arm of the Babylonians, the prophet decided to stay with the very people who had oppressed him, rather than live out his days in the luxury of Babylon.

YOU MAY NEVER SEE a specific outcome to your prayers other than the increasing sense of peace you experience internally. Job got what he needed from God without ever knowing any of the behind-the-scenes events that took place that provoked all the tragedy in his life. The saints of Revelation 6 were given a glimpse of the bigger picture, but perhaps that is only the privilege of those who are already in heaven. Your eventual sense of well-being in this matter is not dependent on what you see, or what you don't see happening—but rather on your increasing confidence in God's sovereignty.

Jesus once told his disciples that he had many things to teach them, but at that particular time, they could not bear the deep implications of those truths (John 16:12). It could be that there is a broader knowledge out there that better explains and answers what has been happening to you — but perhaps God knows that you cannot bear it now, and so that knowledge remains hidden. The only acceptable response to these nonrevealed mysteries is humility and unquestioning submission to a supremely benevolent being who has nothing but your best interests at heart.

Every true prayer has its background and its foreground.

The foreground of prayer is the intense, immediate desire for a certain blessing which seems to be absolutely necessary for the soul to have; the background of prayer is the quiet, earnest desire that the will of God, whatever it may be, should be done.

What a picture is the perfect prayer of Jesus in Gethsemane! In front burns the strong desire to escape death and to live; but behind there stands, calm and strong, the craving of the whole life for the doing of the will of God ...

Leave out the foreground, let there be no expression of the will of him who prays, and there is left a pure submission which is almost fatalism.

Leave out the background, let there be no acceptance of the will of God, and the prayer is only an expression of self-will, a petulant claiming of the uncorrected choice of the one who prays.

Only when the two are there together, *the special desire resting on the universal submission, the universal submission opening into the special desire,* is the picture perfect and the prayer complete.

Phillips Brooks (1835-1893)

If you have taken all these steps leading up to and including the prayer of retribution—and still have not found the sense of well-being and emotional equilibrium that these tools can offer—then it's time to find a professional and competent counselor. He or she may see things that you're missing, so don't hesitate to find the help that you need so that you can find the peace that God promises.

The Script . . .

Here is a series of questions to help you through each step of this process. You can go through and answer these questions by yourself, or have a trusted friend or competent counselor ask them for you. Again, supreme confidentiality must be maintained in this process.

You may be able to settle this issue in a few minutes at the kitchen table, or it may be a process that gets spread out over several years.

How long it takes does not matter. What matters is that you're actively engaged in the process and heading in the right direction.

As we talk, I will frequently bring up this question—"If I were to ask you to forgive this person, what would you say?"

If you're not ready, then just say, "I'm not ready".

If you're not ready, but making progress, then say something like, "I'm not ready yet, but I'm getting closer."

If you are ready, simply say "Yes, I'm convinced that God will keep His promise to accomplish justice on my behalf, and so I am ready to forgive."

Here we go . . .

"What did this person do to you that created a loss for you, damaged your reputation, or caused you pain in some way?"

"If I were to ask you to forgive this person, what would you say?"

"Is it safe for you to confront this person? If so, have you done so? If so, how did it go?"

"If I were to ask you to forgive this person, what would you say?"

Have the appropriate systems of justice, either through the governing authorities or the church, been set in motion? If so, how is that going?

"If I were to ask you to forgive this person, what would you say?"

On a scale of 1 to 10, (with 10 being genuine repentance, and one being remorseless blameshifting) how did the offender react to responsible confrontation?

"If I were to ask you to forgive this person, what would you say?"

"Based on where this person is landing on the scale, what type of relationship, if any, would you expect to have with this person?"

"If I were to ask you to forgive this person, what would you say?"

"How will your level of vulnerability to this person change because of what he or she did and his or her consequent response?"

"If I were to ask you to forgive this person, what would you say?"

"Are you confident that this person, if he or she remains remorseless about what happened, will one day meet with God's earthly and eternal discipline? On a scale of one to ten, how confident are you?"

"If I were to ask you to forgive this person, what would you say?"

"Have you accomplished for yourself the type of acknowledgment and acceptance of responsibility you'd like to see from this other person?

If not, you really need to focus on that before moving forward. When you have, we'll continue."

Is there something you could ask of God, something that you want him to specifically do in this case . . . to remove an emotional obstacle that's preventing you from moving forward . . . to accomplish what you cannot on your own?

If there is, I don't want you to tell me or anybody else. Go ahead and offer those words in the private sanctuary of prayer.

"Now, if I were to ask you to forgive this person, what would you say?"

IF YOU ARE MAKING ANY PROGRESS WHATSOEVER in the process, take some time to rest, regroup, and if necessary, go back to this exercise whenever you're ready.

Epilogue

Passing from Pain to Peace . . .

If you'll indulge me, I'd like to end with a personal story that illustrates the immense relational and reconciling power of acknowledging God's absolute sovereignty over all human disputes . . . which, again, is foundational to our ability to forgive anyone.

One spring, I got a call from my sister saying that Dad had been diagnosed with cancer. Serious, of course, but nothing that couldn't be corrected with surgery. Only two weeks after the diagnosis, Dad was on the operating table. But when the surgeon got to the affected area, he immediately stopped what he was doing. This rare form of cancer had spread so rapidly there was no way that surgery was going to do him any good.

Other possible treatments included chemotherapy and radiation . . . but the disease was so aggressive, and had already done so much damage, that they could only expect the treatment to give him a few more weeks—and he'd be totally miserable the whole time.

So Dad decided to forego any treatment whatsoever.

The doctor asked my father outright . . . "Mr. Schmidt, do you know that you are dying?" To which my father replied, "Yes, I'm passing from pain to peace" . . . and then began to politely interview the doctor about the physician's spiritual health.

After a few weeks, I was able to spend some time around his kitchen table, reminiscing about the past and talking about the granddaughter that he probably wouldn't see . . . at least not in this life. He recorded himself reading some Scripture and children's books so the baby could one day at least hear his love for her. He wanted to be sure that everything was okay between us, and that nothing had been left unaddressed. I assured him that everything was cool between us. He spent a lot of time at that table with his eyes closed and a small smile, with his head nodding at the pleasant thoughts that seemed to be passing through.

When the time came that I absolutely had to leave, a concerned look came over Dad's face. He knew, and I knew, that this might be the last time we saw each other—at least this side of heaven. I assured him, though, that I would do everything in my power to see him again

125

before that time came, and that seemed to reassure him. Of course my step-mom was with him, so he wouldn't be alone.

About a month later, my sister called again. Dad had taken a sudden turn, and he didn't have much time. My pregnant wife (who was eight months along) and our two kids jumped into the car to make the cross-country trip from Colorado to Illinois. Somewhere in Nebraska, I started having second thoughts . . . *Am I going to break my promise to him? Is he going to be gone before I get there? Am I going to be able to say good-bye and tell him I love him?*

Linda and the kids wanted to be there too, and we didn't have the money to fly all of us on such short notice. And, besides, the obstetrician wouldn't let Linda fly. And there was no way I'm going to let her drive cross-country by herself, with the kids, while I cruised on ahead at 36,000 feet.

Not one to keep my anxieties to myself, Linda kept assuring me . . . "We're going to make it, we're going to make it." So I turned around and told the kids —"Sorry guys, no potty breaks . . . we gotta get there."

[Of course, we did stop occasionally, but I had a stopwatch out.]

Fourteen hours later, Linda dropped me off at the hospital entrance, and I made a beeline to the elevator. I didn't bother with a visitor's pass, and I may have stepped on a toe or two in the elevator. When the doors opened, my step-mom and sister were there, waiting to get on. They were both smiling—that most certainly had to mean I wasn't too late. After assuring me that Dad was resting comfortably, they brought me to his room.

He was conscious, but his eyes were closed. He had that same small smile, and his head was nodding at the pleasant thoughts that seemed to be passing through his head.

I held his hand and said, "Hi Dad, this is Doug. I love you."

His mouth was dry, but he managed to say, "I love you too."

I made it.

Dad spent the next twenty-four hours slipping in and out of consciousness. All he seemed to want is for us to be there, and for someone to swab his mouth with orange pop every few minutes. I'd joke with him and say, "Y'know, this is not too good for your teeth." He would smile, and just say "hmmm" with pleasure whenever one of us performed this sacred duty.

At my Dad's bedside, I had to smile to myself when I recalled part of the poem by Dylan Thomas—one that he wrote while his father was on his deathbed . . .

> Do not go gentle into that good night,
> Old age should burn and rave at close of day;
> Rage, rage against the dying of the light.

What a contrast. If my father had the strength, he'd probably be whistling "Zip-a-Dee-Doo-Dah."

For insurance reasons, they had to transfer Dad from the hospital to a private care facility. Appropriately enough, it was called a transition center. When they got to his room, they brought in large, sling-like device and told my Dad that they had to weigh him because he was a new patient. He rolled his eyes, smiled, and cooperated as best he could.

At some point during the day, it dawned on me that Linda and I had lost our first son (Gregory) shortly after he was born on this date nine years ago.

When the morning came, we were all there, and Dad still had the same pattern of breathing. Nothing for about a minute, and then a long inhalation. The hospice nurse had placed a small oxygen tube over his nose, but she said that it was more for our comfort than his. His body was telling us, by the way it was breathing, that it was simply asking for less and less oxygen.

When the end came, my step-mom was holding his hand and committed his spirit to the Lord.

IT'S BEEN SEVERAL YEARS SINCE MY DAD'S DEATH, and I still miss him terribly. In my office, I have a picture of him with my two older kids and my nephew—one that I took during that last extended visit with him.

Of course, as some fathers and sons do, we disagreed strongly about certain issues—most notably, how we all dealt with Mom's manic depression and her boundary-violating behavior. Eventually it came to the point where we knew we weren't going to change each other's minds. After all the difficult work was done, we had to leave it in the Lord's hands. Eventually, God would judge between us.

So now Dad has stood before God, and the issues between us have been settled. When I think about all the challenges we struggled through, the Lord seems to say, "It's taken care of—the arguments are over. I have had the final word." Whether for or against me, somewhere in between, or maybe we were both wrong—I don't know. All that I know for sure is that God has answered the lingering questions, and that has always been enough.

Occasionally though, I'd want to know who "won."
Just what was God's verdict between us?

Whenever I start wondering about this, I'm reminded of one of my Dad's favorite stories from the Gospels. He loved the conversation that Peter and Jesus had when the disciple wanted to know the eventual fate of one of his fellow believers (John 21:21-22).

The Lord's response to Peter seems to be the right words for me whenever I ask God about how Mom and Dad fared on their final examinations.

"What is that to you? You must follow me."

AND WITH THESE WORDS OF JESUS, we end our discussion.
From the friendly disagreements to the emotionally-divisive issues;
From the family spats to the long-term estrangements;
From the bully on the playground to the bully who blows up buildings;
From racial profiling to apartheid;
From hate crimes to the holocaust;
From gender discrimination to genocide;
From the careless comment to the destruction of human life . . .

After we have done all we can legitimately do . . .

God will have the final word.

Pray to this end.